Supporting Children's Reading

A complete short course for teaching assistants, volunteer helpers and parents

Margaret Hughes
and
Peter Guppy

Routledge
Taylor & Francis Group

LONDON AND NEW YORK

First edition published as *On Cue: Helping Children to Read* in 2003
by NASEN

This edition published 2010
by Routledge
2 Park Square, Milton Park, Abingdon, Oxon, OX14 4RN

Simultaneously published in the USA and Canada
by Routledge
270 Madison Avenue, New York, NY 10016

Routledge is an imprint of the Taylor & Francis Group, an informa business

Typeset in Perpetua and Univers by
Keystroke, Tettenhall, Wolverhampton

Printed and bound in Great Britain by
The MPG Books Group

British Library Cataloguing in Publication Data
A catalogue record for this book is available from the British Library

Library of Congress Cataloging-in-Publication Data
Hughes, Margaret.
Supporting children's reading : an INSET course for teaching assistants
and volunteer helpers / Margaret Hughes and Peter Guppy.
p. cm.
Rev. ed. of: On cue : helping children to read / Peter Guppy and Margaret Hughes. 2003.
Includes bibliographical references.
1. Reading (Elementary) 2. Teachers' assistants—Training of.
I. Guppy, Peter, 1944– II. Guppy, Peter, 1944– On cue. III. Title.
LB1573.H924 2010
372.41—dc22   2009030415

ISBN10: 0–415–49836–8 (pbk)
ISBN10: 0–203–86201–5 (ebk)

ISBN13: 978–0–415–49836–4 (pbk)
ISBN13: 978–0–203–86201–8 (ebk)

Contents

Introduction

Reading is one of the most important skills in life. It enables us to find out almost anything, discover new worlds and adventures, and lose ourselves between the covers of a book. No wonder we want it for our children; no wonder so many hours are spent hearing children read. How essential it is, then, that these hours be well spent.

The support children receive on their journey into reading can come from a range of people, both in school and at home – the child's 'reading team'. The more information and guidance this team has, the more secure its members will feel and the more effective they will be. High-quality training is invaluable.

Supporting Children's Reading is a course for teaching assistants and volunteer helpers ('reading buddies'); it is equally valuable as a resource for parents' evenings. There are eight workshops, each about 40 minutes long; some have extra reading to take away. After the sessions, we believe people will feel more confident about answering questions such as:

- How does reading work?
- How do I help a child who is stuck on a word?
- How do I best use phonics?
- How do I know when a book's too hard? And what do I do when it is?
- How exactly does reading *to* a child help?
- Can a book ever be too easy for a child?

Trends in teaching reading come and go, often highlighting one element of reading at the expense of others. However, in *Supporting Children's Reading* we demonstrate that all the elements of reading are necessary, equal and complementary.

Presenter's Guide

How the workshops are set out

- Each workshop comprises a number of screens to be shown to course participants, with accompanying Presenter's Notes.
- These Notes are to support you, the course presenter, in talking through whatever is shown on the screen.
- The Notes for each workshop appear together on the pages following the workshop's screens. Each screen's set of Notes carries the number of the screen to which it refers.

Getting the best out of your presentation

- The Presenter's Notes are *not* verbatim scripts. Rather, they give you the information you need to convey but allow you the freedom to relay it in your own words . . . . by far the most convincing manner of presentation. (This is why the notes are written as 'Explain this' or 'Point out that', etc.)[1]
- To this end, we recommend that you familiarise yourself with the whole course prior to presentation, and 'make it your own'. You will want to shape it to suit the particular experience and needs of your audience and there is generous space on the notes pages for you to annotate.
- It's a good idea to use variety in the way you present the screens – sometimes read out the screen, sometimes allow time for your group to read it for themselves.
- Although the workshops include opportunities for group interaction and discussion (signalled by the icon), you may choose to invite comments, questions and suggestions at any time.

---

1 We use 'adult' as the term for the person supporting the child, as covering teacher, classroom assistant, parent, etc., and as being non-gender-specific. We try to avoid any gender-specificity for the children, too (which sometimes results in tortuous uses of 'the child' or 'children').

Photocopying

- You are free to copy, as an *aide-mémoire*, some or all of the screens for distribution to your groups. *Permission to photocopy and distribute applies to screens only, not to the Presenter's Notes. (For single use only, Presenter's Notes may be copied for ease of workshop delivery.)*
- In the case of certain workshops (e.g. Workshops 3 and 4) some screens are more legible as individual photocopies.
- Additional photocopiable material is listed below.

Additional material

- Screens are also available as PowerPoint slides, downloadable from:

    http://www.routledgeteachers.com/resources/fulton

- In Workshops 3, 4 and 5 there are handouts to be photocopied for your group to take away:

    Workshops 3 and 4 each have two 'teaching tips'.
    Workshop 5 has a reference sheet.

- There is an optional Reading Observation Sheet (ROS), with sample comments (Appendix).

    Note: While available for school use, this ROS could also form the basis of a revision workshop, as an extra to the course.

Diplomacy alert

It is advisable to agree with your course members that they come to you first if they have any questions/issues about your school's policy, organisation and approaches, arising from either the workshops or from their own observations around the school.

WORKSHOP 1

Basics of reading

The balance of clues – Seen and Unseen

Screen 1/1   **Workshop 1**

OUTLINE OF COURSE

Workshop 1   Basics of reading: the balance of clues – Seen and Unseen

Workshop 2   More about clues

Workshop 3   Teaching tips 1–5: phonics backs up meaning

Workshop 4   Teaching tips 6–10: meaning backs up phonics

Workshop 5   Three levels of reading

Workshop 6   Frustration and Independent levels in action

Workshop 7   Instructional level in action

Workshop 8   It's a team game: teaching assistant and teacher

---

PRESENTER'S NOTES FOR WORKSHOP 1

Screen 1/1: Outline of course

● Have Screen 1/1 on display as the group arrives and settles in.

● There may be various 'housekeeping' points to make about fire exits, toilets etc.

● Explain the rationale for providing this course – making the most of their time and energies in ensuring that children are supported effectively and helped to make good progress with their reading.

● Continue with the following points:

  ○ As presenter, having had a close look through the entire course, you can promise that it is based on close scrutiny of what children do when they meet a problem word, and how they can be helped.

  ○ It does this very realistically, examining numerous 'snapshots' of children reading.

  ○ Although each workshop is very full, this should not prevent the group from having an input, asking questions, making observations and discussing points along the way.

● Supplement these opening remarks by distributing to each participant a copy of the Introduction, page 1, backed with a copy of Screen 1/1. (It may be useful to put out the copies beforehand, one on each seat.) Allow time for the group to read the Introduction.

● Draw attention to the titles of the eight workshops, as displayed on the screen. You will probably be able to add dates for each session at this point.

● After that, you are ready to begin this first workshop, by displaying Screen 1/2.

Screen 1/2

BASICS OF READING

The balance of clues – Seen and Unseen

This workshop will show you that:

● we use a range of clues to read a word

● there are two types of clue

   ○ on the page (Seen)
   ○ in your head (Unseen)

● reading a word involves a balance of these two types of clue

● listening to a child read involves

   ○ being aware of clues
   ○ observing the child's use of them.

Screen 1/2: Workshop aims

● Explain that each workshop will begin by setting out its aims.

Here are the aims for this session:

● Allow enough time for the group to read these aims.
● There will be explanation of what is meant by 'Seen' and 'Unseen' as we go on.

Screen 1/3

BEN'S BALANCING ACT

Let's watch nine-year-old Ben tackling the problem word: *phantom*

1. Because I know this is a ghost story, I'm expecting a word to do with ghosts.

2. Because the previous word is 'the', I'm expecting the word to be a noun (the 'something-or-other').

The night was dark, without a moon and given to swirling fog, but he was not afraid as he entered the graveyard, feeling his way from headstone to headstone. As he reached the old chapel, it went colder. Then he saw it – the *phantom*; white and shadowy, with a faint green glow about it.

3. OK. It can't be 'ghost' or 'spirit' because it starts with a 'p'; it looks like *p-han-tom*. P-hantom? Panton? Ah! Ph like in Philip or photo. It's *ph-ant-om*.

5. *Yes*. It's phantom all right. These next few words clinch it.

4. *Phantom!* Like on my DVD!

Supporting Children's Reading, 2nd edn, Routledge © Margaret Hughes and Peter Guppy 2010

Screen 1/3: Ben's balancing act

- Introduce this example as a demonstration of good independent reading.
- Mention that Ben is nine, and through early support has become a confident reader, ready to have a go at new words. Good support is what these workshops are about.
- Ask the group to read the central box only (Ben's text), pointing out that the problem word is *phantom*.
- Read out the surrounding boxes that show Ben's thoughts (in numerical order).
- Explain:

  ○ the fact that his thinking is happening at speed
  ○ that we can't know the exact order of his thoughts.

Screen 1/4

WHAT BEN DID

Ben combined his knowledge of stories, language and ghosts with his knowledge of phonics to complete the puzzle.

Background knowledge told him to expect a noun – a ghostly noun, and phonic knowledge of 'ph' clinched it for him.

Ben was successful in solving that problem word, *phantom*, because he made good use of a range of clues:

On the page

SEEN

In his head

UNSEEN

Screen 1/4: What Ben did

- Read the summary of Ben's reasoning, in the box.
- Point out that Ben's range of clues includes:

  ○ general knowledge
  ○ knowledge of stories
  ○ knowledge of language
  ○ phonics

- Introduce the concept of Seen and Unseen clues – those on the page and those in the head.

A possible question

Q. What if Ben had actually never heard of 'phantom'?

A. ● Your support strategy would be to:

  ○ praise his phonic attempt
  ○ ensure proper pronunciation of *phantom*

- His phonic knowledge plus his use of background knowledge would actually have *added* this new word to his vocabulary (make sure he understands it).
- This session focuses on watching how a good reader works. Other workshops will look at ways to help a child develop the strategies Ben employs.

Screen 1/5

BEN BALANCED TWO TYPES OF CLUE

clues on the page   clues in his head

SEEN   UNSEEN

Neither type of clue works alone.

Each has equal importance.

Each works in conjunction with the other.

Screen 1/5: Ben balanced two types of clue

● Expand on the idea of 'Seen' and 'Unseen', by explaining that:

  ○ the clues on the page are Seen clues; those in your head are Unseen clues;
  ○ both Seen and Unseen are equally important; clues often belong to both 'head' and 'page', often it's not clear cut.

● Read out the three sentences on the screen, and stress their importance.
● Introduce the idea, to be stressed in later workshops, that one clue is never enough.
● Ask the group to hold these ideas in mind, as they look back at Ben's reading of *phantom*.

Screen 1/6

BEN'S BALANCING ACT

Let's watch nine-year-old Ben tackling the problem word: *phantom*

1. Because I know this is a ghost story, I'm expecting a word to do with ghosts.

2. Because the previous word is 'the', I'm expecting the word to be a noun (the 'something-or-other').

3. OK. It can't be 'ghost' or 'spirit' because it starts with a 'p'; it looks like *p-han-tom*. P-hantom? Panton? Ah! Ph like in Philip or photo. It's *ph-ant-om*.

The night was dark, without a moon and given to swirling fog, but he was not afraid as he entered the graveyard, feeling his way from headstone to headstone. As he reached the old chapel, it went colder. Then he saw it – the *phantom*; white and shadowy, with a faint green glow about it.

5. *Yes.* It's phantom all right. These next few words clinch it.

4. *Phantom!* Like on my DVD!

Supporting Children's Reading, 2nd edn, Routledge © Margaret Hughes and Peter Guppy 2010

For Screen 1/6 redisplay Screen 1/3 – Ben's reading of *Phantom*.

● *Ask*:

So, where *did* Ben find his clues for *phantom*?
Were they on the page, or in his own head?

● Read out boxes 1 and 2.

Ask the group which one is a clue on the page and which is a clue in Ben's head.

(Box 1 – on the page; Box 2 – in Ben's head.)

● Read out boxes 3, 4 and 5.

Point out that they are not as clear cut.

Point out their mixture of 'head' clues and 'page' clues.

(Box 3 – knowledge of ghost stories is in Ben's head; the words on the page have told him that this is a ghost story.

Box 4 – the word *the* is a signal on the page, while Ben's knowledge of language pattern is in his head.

Box 5 – the words are on the page; Ben's background knowledge is in his head.)

● **To wind up this discussion, point out again that Ben was balancing the two types of clue.**

Screen 1/7

CAN YOU SPOT THE CLUES BEN USES?

Ben reads:

The *Th . . . Th-ames* flows through the middle of London.

(He pronounces *Th* as in *thumb*, and – *ames* as in *names*.)

Ben: *Th-ames? What's that?*

(Ben rereads the sentence to himself.)

Ben: *Aaah!* flows . . . *It's a river!* . . . flows through London! *It's that river!*

He now reads: The Thames flows through the middle of London.

(This time he pronounces it correctly as *Tems*.)

Every printed page is full of clues – just waiting to be used.

Every reader has clues in his head – just waiting to be used.

So, every person helping children read should be a detective; that is – A CLUE SPOTTER.

Screen 1/7: Can you spot the clues Ben uses?

- Explain that Ben is reading a guide book to London.
- Ask the group, perhaps in twos or threes, to spot the clues Ben uses to read *Thames*.

- After a short time, exchange ideas. Aim to bring out the following points:

  ○ With *Thames* coming so early in the sentence, it seems that Ben has no clues other than the phonics of the word itself.

  ○ But these phonics are not very helpful. After all, *th* is not usually a *t* sound, and *ames* is not usually sounded as *ems*. If he were to meet *Trent* or even *Mississippi*, the phonic clues would be more reliable.

  ○ However, he carries on and takes in information from *flows through* and *middle of London*, which gives him more clues to draw on.

  ○ This allows him to draw on another important clue: his own general knowledge.

  ○ Once armed with the knowledge from all these clues, there is just enough phonic information in *T_ _ m_ s* to clinch it for him. (*And* to teach him a new spelling!)

- Draw attention to the detective, as illustrating that hunting around for clues is the way to solve a problem. Read out the text that accompanies the picture.

A possible question

Q. What if Ben had never heard of the Thames?

A. ● Your support strategy would be:

  ○ praise his phonic attempt
  ○ praise the fact that he knew it was a river
  ○ tell him the word.

- The good use that Ben made of his general knowledge proves just how important such knowledge is. Ben was very unlucky in meeting this word, because Thames offers such unusual phonics as to be almost impossible to build.
- This session focuses on watching how a good reader works. Other workshops will look at ways to help a child develop the strategies Ben employs.

Screen 1/8

THIS WORKSHOP SHOWED THAT

- we use a range of clues to read a word
- there are two types of clue:

  - on the page – Seen
  - in your head – Unseen

- reading a new word involves a balance of these two types of clue
- listening to a child read involves:

  - being aware of clues
  - observing the child's use of them.

Next time you listen to a child reading, try some clue-spotting!

Screen 1/8: Workshop summary

- Recap that this session focused on how a good reader works. Other workshops will look at ways to help a child develop the strategies Ben employs.
- Comment on the suggestion in the box. Next time you hear a child read, try some clue spotting!

WORKSHOP 2

More about clues

Screen 2/1　　　　　　　　　　　　　　　　**Workshop 2**

MORE ABOUT CLUES

This workshop will show you:

● the balance of Seen and Unseen clues

● the kinds of clues within these two types

● the distances readers cover in their search for clues

● that one clue is never enough

● that phonic clues are always involved.

　　　Supporting Children's Reading, 2nd edn, Routledge © Margaret Hughes and Peter Guppy 2010

PRESENTER'S NOTES FOR WORKSHOP 2

Screen 2/1: Workshop aims

- Allow time for reading the screen or handout.
- Explain that this workshop will add detail to what was established in Workshop 1:

  ○ about Seen and Unseen clues
  ○ about where some clues to a problem word may be found.

Screen 2/2

TWO TYPES OF CLUE

Clues in your head – **UNSEEN**

- life experience in general
- vocabulary
- experience of different kinds of reading materials
- experience of different kinds of stories
- experience of different authors' voices
- experience of book-language

Clues on the page – **SEEN**

- pictures
- whole pages, etc.
- paragraphs
- sentences

- strings of words
- whole words
- parts of words (phonics)
- punctuation

Supporting Children's Reading, 2nd edn, Routledge © Margaret Hughes and Peter Guppy 2010

Screen 2/2: Two types of clue

● The two types of clue were introduced in Workshop 1. This time we're considering the different kinds of clue within each type.

● Read out and explain each heading in the Unseen section. You could personalise where appropriate. (You and the group may have anecdotes about children's reactions to the language of particular books.)

Use the following notes for guidance:

○ Life experience in general . . . *general knowledge; human experience.*
○ Vocabulary . . . *words heard, used and understood but new in print (e.g. Ben's 'phantom').*
○ Experience of different kinds of reading materials . . . *books, comics, poems, adverts . . .*
○ Experience of different kinds of stories. . . . *fairy, horror, funny, adventure, fantasy . . .*
○ Experience of different authors' voices . . . *serious, jokey, friendly, formal (e.g. a serious fairy story; a jokey fairy story; an official war report; a soldier's diary).*
○ Experience of book-language . . . *e.g. 'Once upon a time', 'at the far forest's edge', 'however long the road there will be an ending'.*

● Point out that all those hours spent reading to children, talking with them, widening their experience, helps build Unseen clue knowledge. (Workshop 6 looks at this again.)

● Read out the Seen section, pointing out that *all* the headings in this list provide a huge number of clues for any given word.

● As a bridge to the next screen, 2/3, tell the group that now they know what is meant by clues, and have seen a list of what's in each type, they are going to look at some actual cases where children come up against problem words.

● Explain that the next couple of screens will show four examples of problem words on which a child 'stuck'.

CLUE SPOTTING (1) – CLUES BEFORE THE WORD

Where is the clue, relative to the problem word? And how far must the reader travel to find it?

Sometimes, there is a clue *before* the problem word.

Example 1: A clue *just* before the problem word.

> He looked at the clock to see the <u>time</u>.

Example 2: A clue *some distance* before the problem word.

> 'What's that? You're covered in spots! It's not catching, is it?'
> 'No, no. I know you don't want your Leonard getting it. It were bad
>   enough when he had measles, chicken pox and whooping cough. It's
>   just an <u>allergy</u>,' she said.

Screen 2/3: Clue spotting (1) – Clues before the word

- Explain that the questions at the top of the screen are to be kept in mind for all the following examples.
- Point out that the problem words in the examples are underlined.
- Explain that here, in these two examples, the clues come *before* the problem word.

Example 1 – a clue just before the problem word.

- Ask the group to suggest what the clue is in the first example. (This could be the single word 'clock' or the phrase 'looked at the clock', or the phrase, 'looked at the clock to see'.)

Example 2 – a clue some distance before the problem word.

- Ask the group what the clue is in the second example. (This could be the sentences: 'It's not catching, is it?' 'No, no.')
- Note how far this clue comes before the problem word; note also that it is on more than one line.
- Stress that this distance calls for the flexibility to read to and fro – which may need encouragement.
- And stress that this travelling back for a clue, sometimes across several sentences, should never be discouraged, and may very well need to be taught.
- Remind the group that a clue can be more than one word.

CLUE SPOTTING (2) – CLUES AFTER THE WORD

Sometimes, there is a clue *after* the problem word.

Example 3: A clue *just* after the problem word.

> Bill <u>laughed</u>. Hee hee hee.

Example 4: A clue *some distance* after the problem word.

> She lay there, very white, just <u>alive</u>. 'Take her to the castle and tell the women to look after her.'

Screen 2/4: Clue spotting (2) – Clues after the word

● Point out that in these two examples the clues come *after* the problem word.

Example 3 – clues just after the problem word.

● Ask the group to suggest what the clue is in this example ('Hee, hee, hee').
● Point out that readers must be prepared to read

  ○ past the problem word
  ○ and sometimes, not 'just past', but on past a full stop.

Example 4 – clues some distance after the problem word.

● Ask the group to suggest what the clue is in this example ('tell the women to look after her' indicates that 'she' is not dead).
● Point out that this reader, again, was prepared to read beyond a full stop . . . and on, right to the end of the next sentence. On other occasions, a reader might need to travel through a number of sentences, even over on to the next page.
● Reading on should always be encouraged and may very well need to be taught.
● Point out that a clue can be more than one word.
● As the bridge to the next screen, 2/5, comment that the workshop now moves on, from clue spotting, to clue using. They are going to see a child in action, using different clues to work out problem words.

Screen 2/5

CLUES WORKING TOGETHER (1)

Example 1: Philip was stuck on the word *multiplication*:

> Lots of hard <u>multiplication</u> sums were set by the maths teacher.

Philip started with **phonic** clues, **meaning** clues triggered the word, and **phonic** clues finally clinched it.

Screen 2/5: Clues working together (1)

● Ask the group, perhaps in twos or threes first, to consider how Philip got the word, making sure the following points are brought out:

○ Philip built the first syllable: *mul-*.
○ But the length of the word was off-putting.
○ So he decided to read on, to the end of the sentence, searching for further clues.
○ This brought him to the meaning clues *sums* and *maths*.
○ These clues triggered a word he knew – *multiplication*.
○ Returning to the word on the page, he confirmed his idea by matching it against the letters.

● Stress that Philip understood the usefulness of reading on, and moved into that option very quickly.
● Comment that Philip's use of clues demonstrates how clues work together. One clue is never enough.

Screen 2/6

CLUES WORKING TOGETHER (2)

Example 2: Sarah was stuck on the word *piano*.

Sam plays a drum. Jack plays the trumpet. Bill plays the <u>piano</u>.

Sarah started with a **single-letter phonic** clue, went on to search through **meaning** clues, then **phonic clues** clinched it.

Supporting Children's Reading, 2nd edn, Routledge © Margaret Hughes and Peter Guppy 2010

Screen 2/6: Clues working together (2)

● Ask the group, perhaps in twos or threes first, to consider how Sarah got the word, making sure the following points are brought out:

○ Unlike *drum* and *trumpet*, which she was able to build, the phonics of *piano* caused Sarah a problem.

○ There were no clues after the word, no picture, so she mentally went through all the instruments she knew.

○ Only one began with '*p*'. She was able to make a match, even though the phonics were unusual.

● Stress that Sarah understood that the clues in her head could help her with the clues on the page.

● Comment again that this example demonstrates how clues work together.

Screen 2/7

PHONIC CLUES ARE ALWAYS INVOLVED
BUT
THEY NEVER WORK ALONE

MEANING BACKS UP PHONICS

PHONICS BACKS UP MEANING

Supporting Children's Reading, 2nd edn, Routledge © Margaret Hughes and Peter Guppy 2010

Screen 2/7: Phonic clues are always involved but . . .

● Point out that a problem word is usually a problem because of its puzzling phonics. Nevertheless, in it there will be some phonic 'hook' that is recognised. So if readers can move beyond the phonics to find wider clues, they can then return to the problem word, armed with an idea of what could make sense, then use phonic clues to check that the word in their head does match the word on the page.

● It is useful to insert a warning here – that *lengthy* phonic tuition during reading can be counterproductive because it interrupts the flow of meaning. Direct phonic teaching is, of course, absolutely necessary. But it should be kept separate from the reading of continuous passages.

Screen 2/8

MORE ABOUT CLUES

This workshop will show you:

● the balance of Seen and Unseen clues

● the kinds of clues within these two types

● the distances readers cover in their search for clues

● that one clue is never enough

● that phonic clues are always involved.

Supporting Children's Reading, 2nd edn, Routledge © Margaret Hughes and Peter Guppy 2010

For Screen 2/8 redisplay Screen 2/1 – Workshop aims.

● Explain that the six examples they've seen in this workshop highlight the necessity of training children to develop the range of strategies they need if they are to become independent readers.

Workshops 3 and 4 will address this.

WORKSHOP 3

Teaching Tips 1–5

Phonics backs up meaning

Screen 3/1   **Workshop 3**

TEACHING TIPS 1–5

Phonics backs up meaning

This workshop will show you:

● that 'hearing reading' is always active, never passive

● five practical ways to help a reader search for clues when stuck on a word

● the balance of meaning and phonics when working out words.

This workshop includes a handout for further reading.

PRESENTER'S NOTES FOR WORKSHOP 3

Screen 3/1: Workshop aims

- Begin the workshop by explaining that these teaching tips are intended for use in varied teaching situations, across the curriculum.
- There are ten tips altogether: five in Workshop 3, five in Workshop 4.
- Draw attention to the emphasis on active involvement. Comment that the well-used description 'hearing reading' unhelpfully suggests something passive.
- Point out that these teaching tips give practical ways to achieve the balance between meaning and phonics which has been emphasised in the two previous workshops.

Screen 3/2

TWO TYPES OF CLUE

Clues in your head – **UNSEEN**

- life experience in general
- vocabulary
- experience of different kinds of reading materials
- experience of different kinds of stories
- experience of different authors' voices
- experience of book-language

Clues on the page – **SEEN**

- pictures
- whole pages, etc.
- paragraphs
- sentences

- strings of words
- whole words
- parts of words (phonics)
- punctuation

Supporting Children's Reading, 2nd edn, Routledge © Margaret Hughes and Peter Guppy 2010

For Screen 3/2 redisplay Screen 2/2 – Two types of clue.

● Point out that it is a reminder of the range of types of clue, Unseen and Seen.

A possible question.

Q. When people talk about 'context clues', what do they mean?

A. All this Unseen experience on Screen 2/2 forms a bank of knowledge that offers clues for the reading of a word. This is 'context'.

Also, the headings listed under Seen on Screen 2/2, apart from phonics and punctuation, are context.

The ten teaching tips help readers to make best use of context, that is:

● the knowledge they have in their heads (Unseen clues)
● the words they can already read on the page (Seen clues).

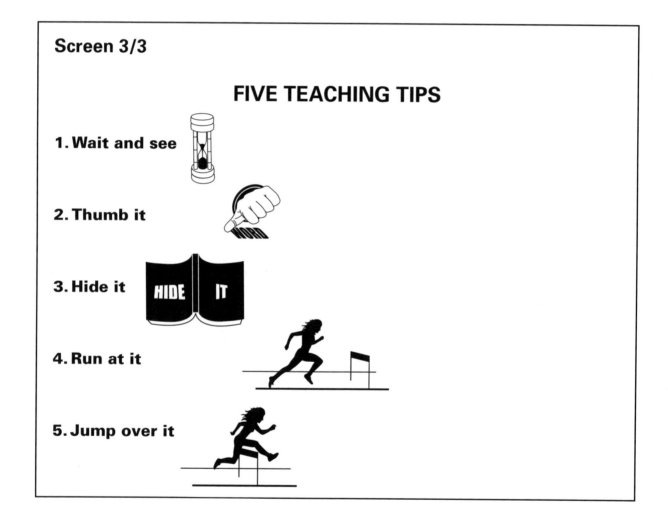

Screen 3/3

FIVE TEACHING TIPS

1. Wait and see

2. Thumb it

3. Hide it   HIDE   IT

4. Run at it

5. Jump over it

Supporting Children's Reading, 2nd edn, Routledge © Margaret Hughes and Peter Guppy 2010

Screen 3/3: Five teaching tips

- As 'hearing reading' is active, this workshop analyses five useful actions for adults to use and teach to readers – 'teaching tips' if you like.
- Explain that for each teaching tip there is a brief 'snapshot' showing the tip in use, with notes on what to do, and why it works.
- Point out that in these 'snapshots' it can be useful for the supporting adult to jot down any observations that might help a teacher plan future work.
- Explain that the workshop itself looks at three of the five teaching tips; tips 4 and 5 are provided as further reading.

Screen 3/4

1. WAIT AND SEE

It was his *wicked* uncle who was king at that time. This bad man had sent Ali to prison, where he stayed for many a long day.

JACK: It was his wickt uncle who was king at the time. This bad man had sent Ali to prison, where . . . *Ah!* (Self-corrects.) . . . **wicked uncle!** *I thought 'wickt' didn't make sense.* (Rereads.) **It was his wicked uncle who was king at** *the* **time . . .**

ADULT: (Quickly and unobtrusively, hardly interrupting.) *Well done. You did that yourself. Good.*

JACK: (Continues.) . . . **This bad man had sent Ali to prison, where he stayed for many a long day.**

(Adult makes a note that Jack needs to know more about -ed endings.)

Screen 3/4: 1. Wait and See

- Explain the layout common to all these examples of readers: the text being read is shown at the top, with the problem word italicised.
- Allow time for the group to read the screen (or their individual copy).

  Note: Individual copies of some screens may be needed throughout this workshop, for better legibility.

- Comment that the group may well be thinking: 'That's odd. We've been told that "hearing reading" means active involvement, and yet the first tip is "Wait and see"!'
- Explain that hanging back and waiting *is* an action, probably the hardest action of all for the adult; but it is extremely important, for two reasons, one for the adult and one for the child.
- Ask the group to discuss, in twos or threes, what these reasons might be.

- After a few moments, bring the group together, and bring out the following reasons:

  - For the adult: unless you're willing to wait you'll never find out just how much the child knows about reading.
  - For the child: readers need the freedom to put into practice what they know.

- Stress that for these reasons 'wait and see' is the most important action of the ten.
- Point out that Jack knew that to read on past a problem word will help him to solve it. (Remind the group of Ben's strategy in Workshop 1, with *phantom* and *Thames*.)

Screen 3/5

1. WAIT AND SEE

What you do

When children continue reading past a misread word, wait, to give them an opportunity to self-correct from information further on in the text.

You will have to decide how long to let the reading go on after the mistake, depending on how much it has changed the sense, or lost the meaning.

Some mistakes – slips of the tongue – may make hardly any difference at all – king at *the* time/king at *that* time – and can usually be ignored; chances are if asked to reread the sentence the reader would self-correct with no trouble at all.

Why 'Wait and see' works

'Wait and see' is not an easy option for the adult. The temptation is to jump in as soon as a mistake is made. But we are working to train children to be independent readers, and the clues to solve a problem word are often further on.

In this example, the adult let Jack keep going over one full stop, and half way into the next sentence; patience which was well rewarded.

Screen 3/5: 1. Wait and see (What you do/why it works)

- Point out that a 'slip of the tongue' error (*the* in place of *that*) was ignored in order to maintain the flow of the reading; this allowed the reader to make best use of context.

- Talk through the following: Jack corrected himself halfway through the next sentence, once he had met further information that defined *wicked*; '*this bad man sent Ali to prison*'. If he hadn't self-corrected, the adult would at some point have stepped in. The adult would not have stepped in immediately after the misreading, because he wanted to allow Jack to do what Jack in fact did – use further context. The intervention could well have waited for two or three sentences, or even the end of the page – allowing Jack a chance to go back for himself.

- Explain that Jack's need to know more about '-ed' endings was noted, in readiness for specific teaching at the right time.

- Emphasise, before moving on, that 'Wait and see' is a genuine, and very important, action. After all, self-correcting after reading on is an action adult readers use all the time.

Screen 3/6

2. THUMB IT

What you do

Cover the problem word with your thumb. Do this from above the word, so as not to hide the next few lines.

Read out the whole sentence to the child, except the problem word.

Say the word s*omething* in place of the problem word, to keep the sentence flowing.

Read as naturally as possible.

(Don't worry: all this takes seconds only.)

Why 'Thumb it' works

Covering the problem word with your thumb draws attention away from the letters of the word and directs it on to wider clues. This puts children in charge of their own problem solving.

There is often a lot of information after the word. In the example you will see next, the problem word is sixth in a nineteen word sentence – giving thirteen more words after it to provide more clues.

Armed with this, the reader can go back to the word. Meaning and phonics can work together. The phonic clues are no longer isolated.

Screen 3/6: 2. Thumb it (What you do/why it works)

- Before displaying Screen 3/6, advise that this teaching tip will be very unfamiliar to some, and may come as a shock, as it asks readers temporarily to ignore the print.
- Display screen 3/6. Note that, here, the what-to-do-and-why screen is presented before its example, to give a clear idea of the tip before it is met in action.
- Explain the value of using the word 'something' instead of a gap for the problem word. 'Something' avoids interruption of the flow of language; and, as you read, it can be given the same intonation and weight as the actual word.

Screen 3/7

2. THUMB IT

> **Mum grew more and more** *anxious* **as darkness fell and still there was no sign of the missing kitten.**

KIM: **Mum grew more and more** . . . (long pause, becoming hypnotised by the letters of the word).

ADULT: (Sensing that the child is not going to read on independently, and seeing the meaning coming up after the word, puts her thumb over the word *anxious*, and reads) **Mum grew more and more** *something* **as darkness fell and still there was no sign of the missing kitten.**

KIM: *Ah, it's like, kind of worried.*

ADULT: *You're absolutely right. She would be worried.*

KIM: *Mmm. (Shakes head.) It's not 'worried', is it?*

ADULT: *Well, the author could have used that word, so you're half-way there. Now I'll take my thumb away. Look again at the word. It starts with ă. Do you know a word that means 'worried' and starts with ă?* (rereads) **Mum grew more and more ă** . . .

KIM: **Anxious.**

ADULT: *Wow! That's brilliant. Funny looking word, isn't it?*

Screen 3/7: 2. Thumb it

- Comment that the group will probably find that Kim's 'hypnotised-by-the-letters-of-the-word' behaviour is a familiar state of affairs. Hence, to break this trance, the temporary removal of the word. But, of course, note that the adult then returns Kim to '*ă*. . .'.

- Point out that in maths, the 'working out' of a problem is valued just as much as getting the right answer; the same applies in reading. Here, the adult knows that much of Kim's learning to read happens during these working-out times.

- Explain that not all children would know the word *anxious*. If, in this situation, Kim had not come up with it, she would have been told it.

- Stress that it's not a crime to tell a word!

- Draw attention to the fact that the adult decided to limit discussion of the phonics of *anxious* to that one simple remark: 'Funny looking word, isn't it?'

Screen 3/8

3. HIDE IT

We'll look around and then *decide* **where you can sleep.**

JASON: (Reading very slowly, word by word.) **We'll. Look. A-round. And. Then.** (Pause.) **d . . . e . . . k . . .**

ADULT: *You're getting too hooked up on single letters again. You're forgetting what the story's about. Now, let's work a bit of magic.* (She takes the book from him.) *I've taken the book away, so you can't even see the word, but I bet, if I read the whole sentence to you, you can still get close to it. Listen. I'll read it nice and quickly. Listen for the meaning:* **We'll look around and then** *something* **where you can sleep.** (Pauses, to give Jason time to think.) *It's OK. I'll read it again:* **We'll look around and then** *something* **where you can sleep.** (**JASON** continues thinking, so adult patiently rereads the sentence a third time.) **We'll look around and then** *something* **where you can sleep.**

JASON: *Is it 'see'?*

ADULT: *Brilliant! Told you you'd get close to it. 'See'* **is** *what the author means, but it's not actually 'see'. This time, instead of 'see', he's used* decide. (She returns book back to Jason, and rereads the whole sentence, pointing to *decide* as it is read.) *You read it now, Jason.*

JASON: **We'll look around and then decide where you can sleep.**

ADULT: *Excellent.*

Supporting Children's Reading, 2nd edn, Routledge © Margaret Hughes and Peter Guppy 2010

Screen 3/8: 3. Hide it

- Introduce Screen 3/8 with 'Let's have a look at another teaching tip along the same lines.'
- Before allowing the group time to read the whole, just read out and comment on the first description of Jason – he's reading slowly, word by word, and letter by letter. Note the adult's next comment: 'You're forgetting what the story's about.'
- Allow time for the group to read the screen or handout.
- In summary, explain that Jason has a habit of reading too slowly to hold meaning, so, to avoid too lengthy a break, *decide* was quite simply given. The flow was maintained and Jason will learn about the phonics later.
- Remind the group that any lengthy break should be avoided, as it interrupts the 'flow' and may result in the reader losing the gist or meaning of the passage.

Screen 3/9

3. HIDE IT

What you do

Take hold of the book yourself, and turn it so that the child can't see the page; repeat the whole sentence, saying the word *something* in place of the problem word. Three or four repetitions may be needed to give the reader sufficient thinking time.

Why 'Hide it' works

Removing the book provides an even bigger break from word-gazing than covering the one single word as in 'Thumb it'.

Like 'Thumb it', it restores the pace and phrasing of natural language, proving to the child that speed is important. It temporarily switches the task from a looking-at-words task to a listening-to-the-meaning task. It is a useful ploy when reading has slowed to a word-by-word pace, and sense has been lost even though each word is read correctly.

Once the overall meaning has been gained, then the reader can return to the look of the word and check his idea using the phonic clue.

Screen 3/9: 3. Hide it (What you do/why it works)

● Ask the group to suggest, in twos or threes, why 'Hide it' works, before Screen 3/9 is displayed.

● After a few moments display Screen 3/9 and allow time for the group to read it.
● Point out that Jason had enough understanding to come up with the word *see*, and, rightly, he was praised for that.
● Explain that if he had not been able to come up with a good alternative, the adult would simply have supplied the word and moved on.
● Stress that it's not a crime to tell a word!

Screen 3/10

TEACHING TIPS 1–5

Phonics backs up meaning

This workshop will show you:

- that 'hearing reading' is always active, never passive

- five practical ways to help a reader search for clues when stuck on a word

- the balance of meaning and phonics when working out words.

This workshop includes a handout for further reading.

For Screen 3/10 redisplay Screen 3/1 – Workshop aims.

● Point out that these 'teaching tip' methods should not be restricted to the reading sessions; they are intended for use in all lessons, across the curriculum.

● Explain that there hasn't been workshop time to look at teaching tips 4 and 5. These are to be taken away today for further reading. (Copy pages 56 and 57.)

● Note that teaching tip no. 4, 'Take another run at it', presents two examples on the one page.

Workshop 3: Further reading 1

Teaching tip 4: Take another run at it

What you do

Reread with natural pace and intonation as far as the problem word, usually from the beginning of the sentence.

Hold and lengthen the word before the problem word, with a questioning note in your voice.

Why 'Take another run at it' Works

Rereading the sentence as far as the problem word works in two ways:

● first, it helps the reader revalue the meaning of important words in the run up to the problem word (see Max);

● second, it acts as a trigger for the right word; this works even when the clues in the run up seem rather 'colourless' – *it; was; in; here; but; I; don't* . . . (see Lee).

Example 1: Max

> **Peter rubbed the puppy dry with a** *towel* **beside the fire.**

MAX: Peter rubbed the puppy dry with a . . . (pause).

ADULT: (Rereads) **Peter** *rubbed* **the puppy** *dry with* **aaaa . . .?** (Stressing **rubbed, dry** and **with**; holding a rising, questioning note on **a**; stopping before **towel**.)

MAX: **Towel!** *I was thinking that said 'two', but it didn't make sense.*

ADULT: *Yes, I can see why you thought that – the same letters are in there – but I'm glad you realised 'two' didn't make sense.*

Example 2: Lee

> **I was told it was in here, but I don't know** *where.*

LEE: (Reading at a word-by-word plod) **I. Was. Told. It. Was. In. Here. But. I. Don't. Know** . . . (pause) . . .

ADULT: (Much more quickly and with conversational intonation) **I was told it was in here, but I don't knooow . . .?** (Her voice rises questioningly on **know**, and she lengthens the word, to hold it.) (Repeats) **I was told it was in here, but I don't knooooow . . .?**

LEE: **Where!** (and he carries on reading the next sentence).

ADULT: *Good* (whispering; hardly interrupting Lee's reading).

PHOTOCOPIABLE RESOURCE

Workshop 3: Further reading 2

Teaching tip 5: Jump over it

What you do

Ask the reader to reread from the beginning of the sentence, to say the word *something* for the problem word, and to read on to the end of the sentence, all at a good pace. Remind the reader that reading at a good pace often helps to get the meaning.

Be prepared to read the sentence yourself, either to demonstrate this action or to support a weary reader. Read with good intonation and at a natural pace.

Why 'Jump over it' Works

As we noticed with 'Thumb it', there is often a lot of help after the problem word. By jumping over the problem word and reading on, the reader not only benefits from the run-up, but is also able to make use of the clues in the rest of the sentence.

Reading at a good pace often helps to get at the meaning.

Example: Ahmed

> **They hid in the barn and the** *deafening* **noise of the machine made them unable to hear anything**.

AHMED: **They hid in the barn and the dee** . . . (pause).

ADULT: *Keep going. Miss it out. You can come back to it.*

AHMED: (Starting again and reading on past the problem word) **They hid in the barn and the** *something* **noise made them unable to hear anything**. (Repeats) **They hid in the barn and the** *something* **noise made them unable to hear anything**. *Is it the same as 'loud'?*

ADULT: *That's it! It means 'loud'. So you know you're looking for a word that means 'loud'. Now you've got the meaning, let's go back to the letters for some more help.*

AHMED: **Deef.** (Pauses) **Deaf!**

ADULT: *The deaf noise? Does that fit? And is it long enough? Look at the word.* (Points to *deafening*.) **The deaf . . . noise**. *Remember you said it meant 'loud'.*

AHMED: **Deafening!**

ADULT: *Well done! And well done for using 'something' when you jumped over the problem word.*

WORKSHOP 4

Teaching tips 6–10

Meaning backs up phonics

Screen 4/1   **Workshop 4**

MEANING BACKS UP PHONICS

This workshop will show you:

● that 'hearing reading' is always active, never passive

● five more practical ways to help a reader search for clues when stuck on a word

● how to focus on the balance of meaning and phonics when working out word

This workshop includes a handout for further reading.

Supporting Children's Reading, 2nd edn, Routledge © Margaret Hughes and Peter Guppy 2010

PRESENTER'S NOTES FOR WORKSHOP 4

Screen 4/1: Workshop aims

- Begin the workshop, as you did for Workshop 3, by explaining that these teaching methods are intended for use in varied teaching situations, across the curriculum.
- Draw attention once again to the emphasis on active involvement when hearing reading.
- Point out again that these teaching tips give practical ways to achieve the balance between meaning and phonics which was emphasised in Workshops 1 and 2.

Screen 4/2

FIVE MORE TEACHING TIPS

6. **Help to build it**

7. **Hint at it**

8. **Rephrase it**

9. **Make a question of it**

10. **Start it**

Screen 4/2: Five more teaching tips

● Explain that this workshop will deal with teaching tips 6, 7 and 8; tips 9 and 10 will be given as further reading.

● Confirm that, as in Workshop 3, for each teaching tip we have an example of the tip in action, with notes on what to do, and why it works.

● Point out again that in these 'snapshots' it can be useful for the supporting adult to jot down any observations that might help a teacher plan future work.

Screen 4/3

6. HELP TO BUILD IT

> **This is a** *cardinal* **beetle.** (This sentence appears as a caption to a picture, without any further text.)

JAMES: *I don't know what that says* (pointing to 'cardinal').

ADULT: *Well, what does that say?* (pointing to 'beetle').

JAMES: (Looking at the picture) **beetle.**

ADULT: *Well now, if that* (pointing to 'cardinal') *is coming in front of* **beetle**, *it's probably telling us something about it.*

JAMES: *It's its name, I think.*

ADULT: *So do I. What kinds of beetle do you know?*

JAMES: *Ladybird . . . cockroach . . . don't know any more . . . Oh! Stag beetle?*

ADULT: *So . . . does that say 'stag'? No. Well, I think because we have no other clues at all . . . it's not as though it's a story . . . we'll have to have a go at building this. See anything in there that you know?*

JAMES: Car . . . card . . .

ADULT: *Go on*

JAMES: Card . . . in . . . al . . . card-in-al . . . cardin **AL**?

ADULT: (Giving pronunciation) **car**dinal. *That's right. Well done.* **This is a cardinal beetle.**

Supporting Children's Reading, 2nd edn, Routledge © Margaret Hughes and Peter Guppy 2010

Screen 4/3: 6. Help to build it

- Allow time for the group to read from the screen or their individual copies.
  Note: Individual copies of some screens may be needed throughout this workshop, for better legibility

- Comment that James has used the only context available to him, and it hasn't got him far enough; nor does he have any prior knowledge to help him (which is often the case with names). Under these particular circumstances, phonic clues are the only clues available.

- Remind the group that they were advised in Workshop 2 that lengthy phonic tuition during reading can be counterproductive, because it interrupts the flow of meaning. Recall examples such as Kim's *anxious* and Jason's *decided*, in Workshop 3, where the adult took care to maintain the flow.

- However, point out that James' sentence was not in a passage of continuous prose, so there was no flow of meaning to be disturbed.

- Let's say the beetle had been a chilopod, and so beyond James' building skills, then the adult would have told him the word.

- **Stress that it's not a crime to tell a word!**

Screen 4/4

6. HELP TO BUILD IT

What you do

Help the child to build the word.

Why 'Help to build it' works

It is useful when meaning clues are hard to find.

It works when the phonics of the word are within the child's grasp.

It can be a way for readers to learn words completely new to them, as James did in our example.

> A cautionary note:
>
> Helping children to build words can be tricky. Any phonic approach must be in line with school guidelines.

Screen 4/4: 6. Help to build it (What you do/why it works)

● Point out that this screen simply sums up the thinking behind the 'Help to build it' tip.
● Draw attention to the cautionary note about the teaching of phonics.

Screen 4/5

7. HINT AT IT

> **Mind you, if our** *enemies* **had been any good they would have finished us off straight away.**

(Stevie was reading this story fluently until this point.)

STEVIE: **Mind you, if our en . . . en . . .** (pause).
ADULT: *They're fighting, remember.*
STEVIE: . . . **enemies!** . . . *yes* . . . **enemies had been any good they would have finished us off straight away** . . . (and he continues to read).

Screen 4/5: 7. Hint at it

● Explain that 'Hint at it' is useful when the reader has used the opening phonics of the word, but is stuck on the rest.

● Ask the group to exchange ideas, in twos or threes, as to why the adult here chose this strategy, and to consider what were its benefits.

● After a few moments, bring the group together, and make sure the following points are brought out.

This adult, knowing Stevie well and impressed by that day's fluency:

○ wanted to keep that reading speed
○ knew the limits of his phonic knowledge
○ wanted to encourage Stevie to always keep the meaning of his reading in mind.

● Point out that 'Hint at it' also works when the reader pauses without making any attempt at the word.

Screen 4/6

7. HINT AT IT

What you do

Give a little reminder about what's been read so far.

Some mention of more general background information may also be of use.

Why 'Hint at it' works

Helping readers recall what has been read so far, or reminding them of the background, are quick ways of making them link meaning with phonics. Such hints need disturb the flow of reading very little.

In the same way, help can come from brief comments to remind readers of their own personal background knowledge; for example: *They've gone angling, don't forget, just like you do* or *What does fire need in order to burn . . . you've just been learning about it?*

Supporting Children's Reading, 2nd edn, Routledge © Margaret Hughes and Peter Guppy 2010

Screen 4/6: 7. Hint at it (What you do/why it works)

- Draw attention to the importance of the comment about disturbing the flow of reading as little as possible.
- Point out that 'Hint at it' is not the same thing as miming clues, or pointing at objects to help readers (e.g. pointing at the 'ceiling' when the child is stuck on that word). The task is to help readers learn how to problem solve by themselves through focusing on clues based solely on the text.

8. REPHRASE IT

We were very poor and couldn't *afford* **a barn.**

SIMON: **We were very poor and couldn't** . . . (pause) . . . ăff (ăff as in 'năff') . . . ăff . . . (pause) . . . ăff- (pause) -ford (pause) a barn (his mispronunciation, ăff-ford, turns the real word into a non-word – he fails to grasp its connection with being poor). *What's that mean?*

ADULT: (Seeing that the problem doesn't lie with the phonics – it lies with the meaning – first of all tries the 'Thumb it' action): **We were very poor and couldn't** *something* **a barn.**

SIMON: **We were very poor and couldn't** . . . (pause) (the 'Thumb it' action hasn't helped here).

ADULT: (Takes the book away, and gives a slight rephrasing of the sentence.) ***We were SO poor we couldn't*** *something* ***a barn.***

SIMON: *Buy?*

ADULT: *Great! Now you've got the point.* (Gives book back again.) *Now look at the word. Look at the opening letters, and listen again:* ***We were so poor we couldn't*** *something* ***a barn.***

SIMON: **Aff . . . Aff . . . Afford!** (Now pronouncing it properly; he returns to the text and reads actual sentence) **We were very poor and couldn't afford a barn.**

Screen 4/7: 8. Rephrase it

- Explain that Simon did all he could – phonic building, reading on, rereading the run-up. He was doing well, actually. And so was the adult, in trying the 'Thumb it' tactic.
- But something in the reasoning of the sentence eluded Simon.
- The adult, realising that he needed to have the meaning brought out, rephrased the sentence. The text was changed from *We were very poor and couldn't . . .* to *We were so poor we couldn't . . .*
- Explain that the change from 'very poor' to the emphasised 'SO poor' happened to bring out the cause and effect which the 'and' of the text had split apart; while the addition of 'we' to 'we couldn't' made it all the more personal, less abstract.
- Reassure the group that rephrasing can be done instinctively and quickly – indeed it usually is. Finer points of grammar stay at the back of one's mind!

8. REPHRASE IT

What you do

Rephrase the sentence and say the word *something* in place of the problem word.

You may need to try various rephrasings until you find one that acts as the trigger for the reader to come up with the right word.

Importantly, having got the problem word, the reader must return to the page and read the sentence as it is actually written.

If you keep a pad and pencil to hand, a rephrasing can sometimes be written out quickly for the reader to see as well as hear.

Why 'Rephrase it' works

The meaning of a sentence can often be phrased in a number of ways. For instance, the sentence:

We were very poor and couldn't afford a barn.

could be rephrased as

We were so poor we couldn't afford a barn.

or

We were very poor so we couldn't afford a barn.

Sometimes, for some readers, one way will make more sense than another.

Quite often, rephrasing is needed to turn 'book language' into more everyday language.

Screen 4/8: 8. Rephrase it (What you do/why it works)

● Read out the **Why 'Rephrase it' works** text, first.

● Remark how straightforward that first sentence seems, to us as adult readers . . . quite often a book-language problem *is* very subtle.

● Add that sometimes the problem arises from a badly written sentence. If this is the case, tell the child so! It can be a confidence booster.

● Allow time for the group to read 'What you do'.

● Encourage the group to feel relaxed about this tip, and just to have a go. It's fun and it's interesting, and it works. A degree in linguistics is not needed!

Screen 4/9

TEN TEACHING TIPS

1. **Wait and see**

2. **Thumb it**

3. **Hide it**

4. **Run at it**

5. **Jump over it**

6. **Help to build it**

7. **Hint at it**

8. **Rephrase it**

9. **Make it a question**

10. **Start it**

Screen 4/9: Ten teaching tips

- Explain that there hasn't been workshop time to look at teaching tips 9 and 10. These are to be taken away today for further reading. (Copy pages 78 and 79.)
- Point out that these methods should not be restricted to the reading sessions; they are intended for use *across* the curriculum.
- Suggest that the list of ten teaching tips could be copied and kept handy, as an *aide-mémoire*.

Screen 4/10

MEANING BACKS UP PHONICS

This workshop will show you:

● that 'hearing reading' is always active, never passive

● five more practical ways to help a reader search for clues when stuck on a word

● how to focus on the balance of meaning and phonics when working out word

This workshop includes a handout for further reading.

Supporting Children's Reading, 2nd edn, Routledge © Margaret Hughes and Peter Guppy 2010

For Screen 4/10 redisplay Screen 4/1 – Workshop aims.

● Note that Workshop 7 will return to these tips.

Workshop 4: Further reading 1

Teaching tip 9: Make a question of it

What you do

Turn a sentence round into a question.

Use as many words from the sentence as you can.

Why 'Make a question of it' works

Making a question out of the actual words of the sentence helps in two ways.

First, it allows you to give the reader a close alternative to the problem word, as with Nat's *think/thought*. Sometimes, you can even plant the actual word into the reader's mind: *What was it that Sam thought about all day long?*

Second, it allows you to point the reader in the right direction (see Ben below).

Such a large amount of help keeps the child's confidence high.

It keeps the reading flowing without too much disruption.

Example 1: Nat

> **The present was sitting on the hall table. Sam** *thought* **about it all day long.**

NAT: **The present was sitting on the hall table. Sam . . .** (pauses).
ADULT: (Quietly, and pretending to be too interested in the story to get hooked up on a problem word.) *What did Sam think about all day long?* (She is actually giving him the problem word, even though it's in a different form: think/thought.)
NAT: *His present.*
ADULT: *Yup. So . . .* (points to word *thought*) *What did Sam think about all day long?* **Sam th . . .**
NAT: **Sam thought about it all day long.**

Example 2: Ben

> **He saw an old nest,** *high* **up in the green branches.**

BEN: **He saw an old nest . . .** (pauses).
ADULT: *Where did he see an old nest?* (By asking a 'where' question, she leads him to see that the rest of the sentence is about place, or position.)
BEN: *Oh! . . .* **high up in the green branches.**

Supporting Children's Reading, 2nd edn, Routledge © Margaret Hughes and Peter Guppy 2010

Workshop 4: Further reading 2

Teaching tip 10: Start it

What you do

Reread up to the problem word, and start building it, using one or more of its initial sounds.

If this is not enough to trigger the word, once again reread up to the word, again build the first part, but this time read on to the end of the sentence.

Why 'Start it' works

Using phonics and meaning together in this way is a very good example of what is meant by balancing the clues.

The phonics is provided by building the beginning of the word.

The meaning is provided by the natural reading of the words around the problem word.

The reader brings both together to clinch the word.

Example 1: Fran

> **She opened the box and** *suddenly* **a jack-in-the-box popped out!**

FRAN: **She opened the box and s . . s . . . s . . .**
ADULT: *Miss that out. Keep going.*
FRAN: (Distracted by the problem, reading quite flatly) **A. Jack. In. The. Box. Popped. Out..**
ADULT: (Reads the whole sentence at a normal pace, and builds a part of the problem
   word.) **She opened the box and s-ud-, sud . . . a jack-in-the-box popped out!**
   (repeats) **She opened the box and s-ud-, sud . . . a jack-in-the-box popped out!**
FRAN: Suddenly! . . . suddenly a jack-in-the-box popped out.

Example 2: Neal

> **When his parents asked what he was doing, Mallory replied 'Well, it's** *obvious,*
> **isn't it? I'm building a robot'**

NEAL: **When his parents asked him what he was doing, Mallory replied 'Well,**
   it's . . ? (pause) *Mmmmm . . .* **ob . . . obv . . .** (pause) **Well it's obv . . .** (pause).
ADULT: (Aware that 'obv' is not a letter-string usually found in English, but not
   commenting on that.) *Good thinking, Neal. I can see you're trying your run-up again, with a
   clever bit of building so far. Read a bit further, see if that helps.*
NEAL: **. . . 'Well it's obv . . . isn't it' – obvious!**

WORKSHOP 5

Three levels of reading

Screen 5/1   **Workshop 5**

THREE LEVELS OF READING

This workshop will show you:

- the three reading levels:

  ○ Independent: books read with ease

  ○ Instructional: books read with support

  ○ Frustration: books to listen to

- that each level makes a vital contribution to reading development

- how to gauge the level of any book for any reader

This workshop includes a handout for further reading.

PRESENTER'S NOTES FOR WORKSHOP 5

Screen 5/1: Workshop aims

- Remind the group that so far they've had four workshops about clue-spotting, and the use of clues.
- However, all that work hinges on the understanding that will come from this session.
- Read out Screen 5/1 and explain that:

  ○ all readers, adults and children, operate at three different levels, all the time, throughout life

  ○ this session will explain what these levels are, and how to recognise them

  ○ each level requires a different form of support, which you'll see in Workshops 6 and 7

  ○ a good weekly reading diet comprises *all* three levels.

Screen 5/2

THE THREE READING LEVELS

Independent level: I can read this on my own

Instructional level: I can read this with help

Frustration level: I need this read to me

Screen 5/2: The three reading levels

● Allow a brief amount of time to read, emphasising that the whole idea applies to all readers, adults and children alike. We all have three levels.

Screen 5/3

SO WHAT HAVE YOU BEEN READING LATELY?

1. tax form
2. holiday insurance policy
3. free newspaper
4. instructions on building flat-pack furniture
5. 'You have definitely won £60,000 . . . (*provided that . . .*)'
6. opening offer from new restaurant
7. helping with child's textbook for homework
8. computer manual
9. knitting pattern
10. own choice holiday reading
11. car manual
12. letter from friend

Independent	Instructional	Frustration
I can read this on my own	I can read this with help	I need this read to me *or, for adults, 'explained to me'*

Supporting Children's Reading, 2nd edn, Routledge © Margaret Hughes and Peter Guppy 2010

Screen 5/3: So what have you been reading lately?

- Introduce this screen as being a demonstration, through looking at what we ourselves have been reading lately, of the fact that we all have three levels.
- Explain to the group that the screen shows a list of everyday reading matter, and a column for each level.

- Ask each person to jot down in which column each item belongs, for them personally.
- When the group has finished, encourage a short discussion comparing their choices, either in twos or threes, or whole-group.
- Point out that different people may well classify the same items differently. For instance, the tax form – for most people this is Frustration, but not if you're a tax inspector.
- Pose the question: 'How does your behaviour alter when reading material in each different column?'

   Independent: I'm fine on my own . . . I'm relaxed . . . no help needed . . .

   Instructional: I need a bit of help with this; I'll ask someone about the bit that bothers me; or maybe consult the dictionary.

   Frustration: I simply can't cope with this; if I really need it, I'll ask someone who knows . . . if I don't, I'll ignore it.

- Point out how our motivation differs from column to column, e.g. ask 'For how long are you happy to go on reading at each level?' It's the same for children!

Screen 5/4

CHILDREN NEED ALL THREE LEVELS

AT THEIR INDEPENDENT LEVEL:

Books read with ease

AT THEIR INSTRUCTIONAL LEVEL:

Books read with support

AT THEIR FRUSTRATION LEVEL:

Books to listen to

Each level contributes to reading development.

Supporting Children's Reading, 2nd edn, Routledge © Margaret Hughes and Peter Guppy 2010

Screen 5/4: Children need all three levels

● Reassure the group that the following ideas appear on a handout for this session. The ideas will be revisited in detail in Workshops 6 and 7.

● Explain each heading, by bringing out the following points:

For Independent level

○ this level is just as important as the other two

○ there are so few problem words at this level that children can read fluently for themselves; and those very few problem words are surrounded by accessible clues

○ children get the chance to practise the skills they've learned, which builds confidence, and makes them feel they've arrived as readers.

For Instructional level

○ this is the level you've met in the 'snapshots' in the previous workshops

○ it is the cutting edge for teaching and learning how to use clues

○ the child must be supported in tackling this more difficult level.

For Frustration level

○ this level, again, is just as important as the other two

○ adults take over the reading, so that the child can meet complex language and ideas

○ it's well out of the child's reading range, because problem words are so frequent that there's insufficient context between them to provide the necessary clues

○ but it *is* well within the child's interest range.

● Explain that children need all three levels all the time. Stress the importance of 'all the time', pointing out that it means that in any one week, or even day, a child should experience all three levels.

● Warn against any notion that the levels are sequential – they're not; they run in parallel. (This is demonstrated in Workshop 8.)

Screen 5/5

HOW CAN WE MEASURE EACH LEVEL?

This is easily done by counting the
unknown words in a passage of about 100 words

INDEPENDENT
0–2 unknown words per 100
can be read by child alone

INSTRUCTIONAL
2–7 unknown words per 100
read by child to adult

FRUSTRATION
10 or more unknown words per 100
read by adult to child

Supporting Children's Reading, 2nd edn, Routledge © Margaret Hughes and Peter Guppy 2010

Screen 5/5: How can we measure each level?

- Point out that at the beginning of the workshop they had a go at grading their own reading materials intuitively. But it is clear that when we grade children's material we need something more than intuition.
- Display Screen 5/5, introducing it with: 'Fortunately, there is a tried and tested formula.'
- Read out Screen 5/5, explaining that the passage doesn't have to be exactly 100 words; take it to the nearest full-stop.
- Emphasise the significance of the names of these three levels. They describe the working relationship between child, book and adult. You may need to explain the label 'Frustration' – it describes how a reader feels if attempting something impossibly difficult.
- Point out the implications of these three levels for the working relationships between the child and adult (e.g. read by adult, read by child). Stress that the ability to recognise these different relationships is crucial when helping children to develop as readers.

Screen 5/6

HOW DOES READING AT DIFFERENT LEVELS CONTRIBUTE TO A CHILD'S DEVELOPMENT?

1. Children can read fluently for themselves.
2. They receive instruction on how to tackle problem words.
3. They hear more complex language, which helps them handle more difficult reading material in the future.
4. Through this wider experience, children become hooked on books.
5. Children are supported as they read more difficult books.
6. Children can feel they've arrived as readers.
7. Adults take over the reading so that children can meet more demanding books.
8. When there are a few problem words, children can still use the clues available when supported by an adult.
9. Children practise what they already know about reading, and build confidence.
10. Children meet facts, situations and ideas matching their interest level.

At Independent level _____

At Instructional level _____

At Frustration level _____

Screen 5/6: How does reading at different levels contribute to a child's development?

● Introduce Screen 5/6 as an activity to help the group get to grips with these three levels; that is, what each level contributes to reading development.

● Display Screen 5/6

● Explain that it shows ten sentences describing the benefits to the child of each level.

● Ask the group in twos or threes to jot down the sentences' numbers against the three headings at the foot of the screen – Independent, Instructional, Frustration – according to where the sentences fit.

● Once the group have done this, discuss their answers – suggesting the following:

   At Independent level – 1, 9, 6
   At Instructional level – 2, 5, 8
   At Frustration level – 3, 4, 7, 10

Note: Answers 9 and 10 are not clear-cut. For example, 9 applies to some extent to Instructional level, and 10 applies to some extent to all three levels. This could make for useful discussion.

● Finally, reassure the group that they will be given some notes to take away, describing the benefits of each level in more detail.

Screen 5/7

JACK'S THREE READING LEVELS

JACK'S INDEPENDENT LEVEL – where nearly all the words can be read

Frog and Toad went out to fly a kite. They went to a large ■■■■■■ (*meadow*) where the wind was strong.

'Our kite will fly up and up,' said Frog. 'It will fly all the way up to the top of the sky.'

'Toad,' said Frog, 'I will hold the ball of string. You will hold the kite and run.' Toad ran across the grass. He ran as fast as his short legs could carry him. The kite went up in the air. It fell to the ground with a bump. Toad heard ■■■■■■■■ (*laughter*). Three birds were sitting in a bush.

JACK'S INSTRUCTIONAL LEVEL – where quite a few words cannot be read

Tim got slowly out of bed. His ■■■■■■ (*throat*) hurt. When he washed his face, he found that his neck hurt a bit, too, if he ■■■■■■■ (*pressed*) it. Tim pulled on his ■■■■■■■ (*clothes*). He must get Sebastian outside before anyone saw him.

He ■■■■■■ (*tucked*) a sleepy Sebastian under his jacket. He was just going downstairs when he remembered the box. He couldn't leave that in his room. He put Sebastian back on the bed, and got out an old ■■■■■■■■■■■■■ (*canvas shoulder*) bag and slipped it on his ■■■■■■■■ (*shoulder*). Then he picked Sebastian up again.

JACK'S FRUSTRATION LEVEL – where very many words cannot be read

He unbolted the door and was in the act of entering the sty with a bucket of food when he suddenly saw an old rat that stood up on its ■■■■■■■■ (*hindlegs*) on the wall and ■■■■■■■■ ■■■■■ (*actually bared*) its yellow teeth at him in the most ■■■■■■■ (*impudent*) and ■■■■■■■■■ (*provoking*) manner ■■■■■■■■■■ (*imaginable*). ■■■■■■■ (*Angrily*) the man looked about for a stick or stone, but by the time he found something the rat had vanished. ■■■■■■■ (*Cursing*) the cheek of the ■■■■■■■■ (*creature*), he pulled the door shut and fed the ■■■ (*sow*) and her litter, never ■■■■■■■■ (*noticing*) that the ■■■■■ (*tally*) of pushing, shoving, squealing, gobbling little lords and ladies now numbered only nine.

Screen 5/7: Jack's three reading levels

● Quickly make it clear that the important thing about this screen is the visual impression – it's not necessary to read it, or to work out what the missing words are – just take in at a glance the impact of the blanks.

● Screen 5/7 gives a visual impression of what Jack's three levels look like, if we blank out the unknown words in passages of about 100 words.

● Warn of the dangers in asking a child to read at Frustration level as though it were Instructional, Instructional as though it were Independent, and dismissing Independent altogether as 'too easy'. In that first case, children are faced with the impossible; in the second case they are asked to struggle through books that are too hard, and in the third case they are denied enjoyable reading.

Emphasise that the correct match of child, book and reading task is vital.

Screen 5/8

ONE PASSAGE, THREE CHILDREN, THREE DIFFERENT READING LEVELS . . .

ROSIE'S INDEPENDENT LEVEL

Tim got slowly out of bed. His ■■■■■■ hurt. When he washed his face, he found that his neck hurt a bit, too, if he pressed it. Tim pulled on his clothes. He must get Sebastian outside before anyone saw him.

He tucked a sleepy Sebastian under his jacket. He was just going downstairs when he remembered the box. He couldn't leave that in his room. He put Sebastian back on the bed, and got out an old canvas shoulder bag and slipped it on his shoulder. Then he picked Sebastian up again.

JACK'S INSTRUCTIONAL LEVEL

Tim got slowly out of bed. His ■■■■■■ hurt. When he washed his face, he found that his neck hurt a bit, too, if he pressed it. Tim pulled on his ■■■■■■. He must get Sebastian outside before anyone saw him. He ■■■■■■ a sleepy Sebastian under his jacket. He was just going downstairs when he remembered the box. He couldn't leave that in his room. He put Sebastian back on the bed, and got out an old canvas ■■■■■■■ bag and slipped it on his ■■■■■■■. Then he picked Sebastian up again.

KATE'S FRUSTRATION LEVEL

Tim got ■■■■■■ out of bed. His ■■■■■■ hurt. When he ■■■■■■ his ■■■■ he ■■■■■ that his neck hurt a bit, too, if he ■■■■■■■ it. Tim pulled on his ■■■■■■■. He must get ■■■■■■■■■ outside before anyone saw him. He ■■■■■■ a sleepy Sebastian under his jacket. He was just going downstairs when he ■■■■■■■■■ the box. He ■■■■■■■ leave that in his room. He put Sebastian back on the bed, and got out an old ■■■■■■ ■■■■■■■■ bag and slipped it on his ■■■■■■■■. Then he picked ■■■■■■■■■ up again.

Screen 5/8: One passage, three children, three different . . .

● Reassure the group that, as for the previous screen, they need not struggle to read every word. Once again, it's the overall visual impact that counts.

● Explain that it shows one passage, presented to three children with very different reading abilities in the same class. For Rosie, it's her Independent level; for Jack, it's his Instructional level; for Kate, it's her Frustration level.

● Make it clear that these levels describe only the reader's ability to cope with the particular book. They make sense only when applied to the match between reader and book.

● Go on to explain that once the level of a book for a particular child has been recognised, the next step is to match up the reading task. So, for these three children here, it was like this: Rosie could read it all by herself; Jack needed support from an adult; Kate needed it to be read to her.

● Ask the group to imagine the difficulties that would have been created if these levels had been mis-recognised . . . If Kate were asked to read the book as if it were Instructional level, imagine her reactions – she would simply give up . . . If Jack were left to read it as if it were his Independent level, he'd learn to equate reading with failure . . .

● Stress that, quite clearly, the match between reader, book and type of support has to be correct. (The handout shows why this match has to be correct.)

Screen 5/9

THREE LEVELS OF READING

This workshop will show you:

- the three reading levels:

- Independent: books read with ease

- Instructional: books read with support

- Frustration: books to listen to

- that each level makes a vital contribution to reading development

- how to gauge the level of any book for any reader

This workshop includes a handout for further reading.

Supporting Children's Reading, 2nd edn, Routledge © Margaret Hughes and Peter Guppy 2010

For Screen 5/9 redisplay Screen 5/1 – Workshop aims.

● Give out the two-page handout *Children Need All Three Levels* (copy pages 98 and 99). Ask the group to read it before the next workshop and to practise recognising the three levels in action around the school.

NOTE: See 'Diplomacy alert', page 3.

Workshop 5: Further reading 1

Children need all three levels

Independent level: books read with ease

Children can read fluently for themselves. They enjoy themselves. Not only that, they also practise what they already know about reading, build confidence, and feel they've arrived as readers.

Instructional level: books read with support

Children are supported as they read a more difficult book. They receive instruction on how to tackle problem words. They learn just how many clues they can use, from pictures, from printed words, from their knowledge of books and life.

Frustration level: books to listen to

Children would be frustrated if they tried to read books at this level; there would be too many unfamiliar words and they wouldn't be able to understand the story or text. Adults take over the reading of these books so that children can meet more demanding text. They hear more complex language, which helps them handle more difficult reading material in the future. Also they meet facts, situations and ideas matching their interest level. Such books act like trailers for forthcoming attractions. Through this wider experience, children become hooked on books.

These levels are based on the ratio of readable words to problem works.

Supporting Children's Reading, 2nd edn, Routledge © Margaret Hughes and Peter Guppy 2010

Workshop 5: Further reading 2

Ratio of readable words to problem words

We cannot expect a learner to develop in the use of clues, if the material is so difficult that it lacks the right amount of known words to provide clues for tackling the problem words.

Independent level: 0–2 unknown words per 100

- Independent level has clues in abundance.

Instructional level: 2–7 unknown words per 100

- Instructional level retains just enough context to provide the necessary proportion of clues to tackle any problem words.

Frustration level: 10 or more unknown words per 100

- Frustration level has so many problem words it has lost the necessary proportion of clues.

WORKSHOP 6

Frustration and Independent levels in action

Supporting Children's Reading, 2nd edn, Routledge © Margaret Hughes and Peter Guppy 2010

PRESENTER'S NOTES FOR WORKSHOP 6

Screen 6/1: Workshop aims

- Remind the group that they were introduced to the three reading levels in the previous workshop – Independent, Instructional and Frustration. Mention the handout they were given, and allow time for discussion and feedback.
- Explain that this workshop will be looking at two of the three levels – Frustration and Independent. The third, Instructional, will be dealt with in the next workshop, Workshop 7.

Screen 6/2

Frustration level: *books to listen to*
Adults take over the reading so that children can meet more demanding books. They hear more complex language, which helps them handle more difficult reading material in the future; they meet facts, situations and ideas matching their interest level. Such books act like trailers for forthcoming attractions. Through this wider experience children become hooked on books.

Independent level: *books read with ease*
Children can read fluently for themselves. They enjoy themselves. Not only that, they also practise what they already know about reading, build confidence and feel they've arrived as readers.

Surprisingly
Frustration and Independent levels *share* two important characteristics:

1. They free children from the mechanics of reading, allowing them to concentrate on meaning.
2. They allow children to develop deeper understandings about books and about themselves as readers.

Screen 6/2: Frustration level and Independent level

● Display Screen 6/2, but cover the two numbered sentences.

● To revise the two levels, read out the two paragraphs from the screen (Frustration level; Independent level).

● Comment that, perhaps surprisingly, there are good reasons for looking at these two levels together.

● Ask the group, in twos or threes, to consider what these reasons might be.

● After a few moments, bring the group together, and make sure the following reasons are brought out:

  ○ What is surprising is the fact that these two dramatically different levels share anything at all! After all, one has clues in abundance, the other has virtually none. One is read easily by the child, the other demands to be read by the adult. (Remind the group of their handout from Workshop 5: *Ratio of readable words to problem words*.)

  ○ But the two levels share these characteristics:

    1. Both free children from the mechanics of reading, allowing them to concentrate completely on meaning.
    2. Both allow children to develop deeper understandings about books and about themselves as readers.

● Comment that at both levels it may seem that the child is having an easy time. But there is more going on than one might think. So neither level is a soft option. This session will demonstrate why.

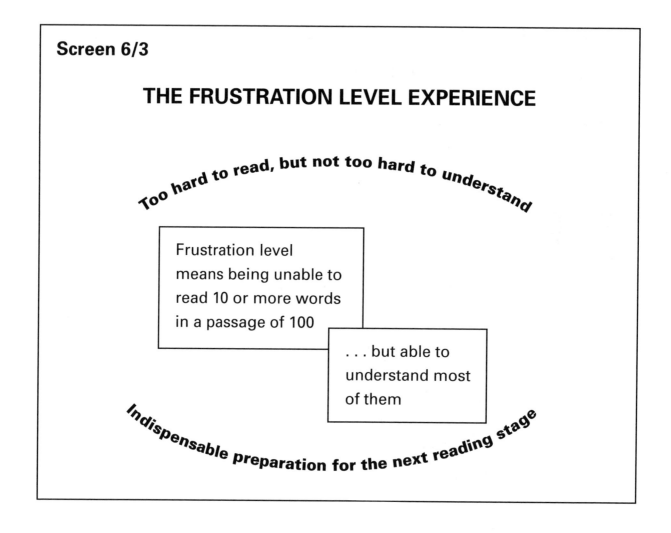

Screen 6/3

THE FRUSTRATION LEVEL EXPERIENCE

Too hard to read, but not too hard to understand

Frustration level means being unable to read 10 or more words in a passage of 100

. . . but able to understand most of them

Indispensable preparation for the next reading stage

Supporting Children's Reading, 2nd edn, Routledge © Margaret Hughes and Peter Guppy 2010

Screen 6/3: The Frustration level experience

● Comment on the name for this level – Frustration – pointing out that it describes how a reader feels if left to struggle alone with this level of text. But **hearing** this level of text is a vital part of any child's reading development.

● Allow time for the group to read the screen.

● Point to 'indispensable preparation' (bottom of the screen) and comment that the next screen explains how listening to difficult books helps a child move on.

Screen 6/4

WHY LISTENING TO DIFFICULT BOOKS HELPS A CHILD MOVE ON

- it introduces essential experience of more complex language, both in words and style; more sophisticated book-language

- it introduces essential experience of a wide range of different kinds of reading materials

- it offers a match with the child's maturity and understanding

- it gets children hooked on books.

Screen 6/4: Why listening to difficult books helps a child move on

● Read out the first bullet point. Advise the group to think about language development through the enjoyment of good books.

● Read out the second bullet point. Point out that this range could be as wide as, for instance, Allan Ahlberg to Alan Bennett, Dahl to Dickens, Beatrix Potter to Harry Potter, from Mole to Adrian Mole, the Discworld to the natural world, steam engines to space travel, Gulliver's Travels to Palin's travels.

● Read out the third bullet point. Comment that one example under this heading is the useful link between books and their screen versions, between films and their printed spin-offs.

● Read out the last bullet point. Point out that being hooked on books matters, because to be good at anything, you have to want to do it.

Screen 6/5

FRUSTRATION LEVEL EXPERIENCE: MAKING IT WORK

HOW? Try to avoid a 'flat' read – have fun, let yourself go.

WHAT? Cover a wide range of materials – some chosen by the child, some introduced by the adult.

WHEN? Make sure that children listen to a variety of books regularly, from the very young non-reader to the older, competent reader.

WHERE? At home and at school (and in the park, the playground, waiting for trains).

Supporting Children's Reading, 2nd edn, Routledge © Margaret Hughes and Peter Guppy 2010

Screen 6/5: Frustration level experience: making it work

● Point to the HOW? section

○ Reassure the group that they don't need to be a trained actor to do this! Even the mildest attempt to liven up one's reading does have an effect. (Shout the shouts, whisper the whispers . . .) It helps if you can get to know the book beforehand.

● Point to the WHAT? section

○ Talk through the following:

An equal partnership in choice of material ensures that on the one hand the child gets the benefits of choosing, on the other, the adult is able to steer the reader into new territory. Such a partnership produces the widest range of materials, e.g. fiction, non-fiction, poetry, instructions, history books, science books, magazines, comics, etc.

● Point to the WHEN? section

○ Caution that, for some children, this experience ends all too soon; that is, once they are judged to be 'readers'.

● Point to the question WHERE?

○ Point out that, in the case of school, listening to text being read in a group or class happens very frequently, not only at story time or in English lessons, but right across the curriculum.

● Mention possible one-to-one opportunities in school:

The time allocated for a classroom assistant to work with an individual child may sometimes be better spent on reading *to* the child than listening to him.

Textbooks and worksheets are often at Frustration level for some pupils. A pre-lesson reading of these materials at some point before the lesson enables these pupils to participate. It could be done by a classroom assistant, say, or perhaps an older pupil (as part of their PSHE (Personal, Social and Health Education)).

Commercial or school-made audio recordings of books are also a useful resource.

Note: If you are adapting this session for a parents' evening, this is a good point to include advice on reading at home. (Schools usually do have their own well-prepared guidelines; for instance, on timing: don't allow reading a book together to have to compete with watching a favourite TV programme, etc.)

Screen 6/6

LONG-TERM INVESTMENT

**Reading to children at their Frustration
level is a long-term investment.**

The pay-off is in the future

If you want children to be readers, read to them!

Supporting Children's Reading, 2nd edn, Routledge © Margaret Hughes and Peter Guppy 2010

Screen 6/6: Long-term investment

● Stress that, even when children can read more books for themselves, it is essential that they continue to hear books and other reading matter read to them. It's vital work. The benefits may not be immediate, but will eventually appear in a variety of ways. Some will be quite specific such as better intonation when reading aloud; a turn of phrase, in writing. Others will be broader in nature:

  ○ a wider spoken and written vocabulary
  ○ an increased interest in words
  ○ a continuing enthusiasm for reading
  ○ increased enjoyment and competence in writing.

● Offer the group this encouraging thought: when children aspire to be star footballers, singers, doctors, racing drivers, they have had before them examples of the 'finished products' as role models. If they are to be star readers, we must be their role models.

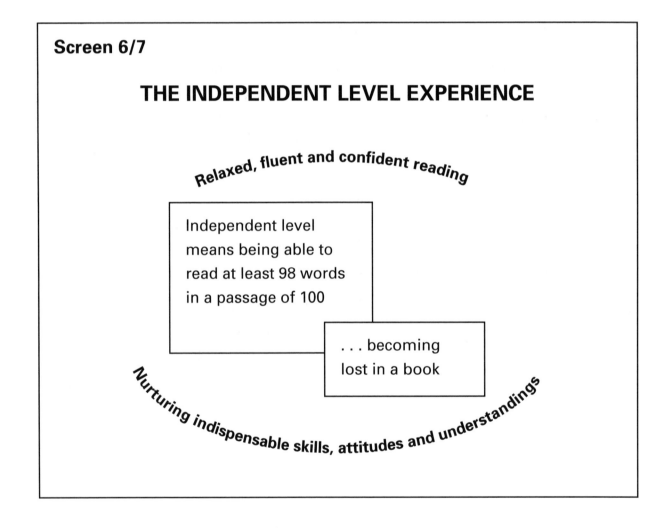

Screen 6/7

THE INDEPENDENT LEVEL EXPERIENCE

Relaxed, fluent and confident reading

Independent level means being able to read at least 98 words in a passage of 100

. . . becoming lost in a book

Nurturing indispensable skills, attitudes and understandings

Screen 6/7: The independent level experience

- Comment that this session now moves on to thinking about the Independent level.
- Allow time for the group to read the screen.
- Bring out the point that, for children, Independent level reading means being independent of support – the only one of the three levels where this happens.
- Point out that some adults dismiss Independent level reading as unchallenging ('too easy'). But in fact, a great deal of learning about reading is taking place.
- Point to 'skills, attitudes and understandings' and comment that the next screen expands on this.

Screen 6/8

WHY READING EASY BOOKS
HELPS A CHILD MOVE ON

● Independent level reading provides the true experience of reading, that is, being fully absorbed in the content, hardly aware of 'the black marks on the page'.

● It builds the child's self-image.

● It puts the child in control.

● It allows consolidation of existing skills.

● It gives the option of successfully reading aloud.

● It permits some choice.

● It builds reading stamina.

● It makes children feel they belong to 'the literacy club'.

Screen 6/8: Why reading easy books helps a child move on

● Emphasise the importance of these positive skills, attitudes and understandings.

● Advise the group again to be wary of any tendency to dismiss this level as not contributing to reading development. Comments such as 'These books are getting too easy for you – you should be reading something harder', are completely misguided. (Harder books are, of course, tackled in the child's Instructional level sessions.)

● Remind the group that, because Independent level reading means using clues intuitively, adults should view it with pleasure, and praise it. This is 'the true experience of reading', being fully absorbed in the content, as though on automatic pilot.

● Expand on 'the literacy club', by noting how, in the first instance, children enjoy knowing they have arrived as readers, and how print then continues to be an important part of their lives. For instance, they want to talk about something they've read, want to recommend a book to a friend, want to read a book to an adult, want to look things up, want to comment on their favourite story or author.

Screen 6/9

INDEPENDENT LEVEL EXPERIENCE: MAKING IT WORK

HOW?

- Let children know that it's OK to be reading at this level . . . adults do.

- Encourage them to relax, have fun, and chat about books . . . adults do.

- Ensure that any discussion you have with them about a book is relaxed and friendly (don't quiz).

WHAT?

- A wide selection of books is needed at this level, for browsing and choosing, at school, and, as far as possible, at home

WHERE AND WHEN?

- Organise a place and a time for the child to sit and read undisturbed; this applies both at school, and, as far as possible, at home.

Supporting Children's Reading, 2nd edn, Routledge © Margaret Hughes and Peter Guppy 2010

Screen 6/9: Independent level experience: making it work

- Remind the group that the Independent level means being able to read at least 98 words in any 100.

- Read out the HOW? section, adding the following points

  ○ Adults have a comfort-zone reading level, and so do children. It's as important at age 5 as at 95!

  ○ Adults chat about things read, recommend books and authors . . . even join book clubs – so should children.

  ○ If you're going to have a discussion with a child about a book:

    ○ it helps to have as much prior knowledge of the book as you can
    ○ be careful not to ask questions about every single book.

- Read out the rest of the screen. If time allows, you could discuss some favourite books and look at a selection. It's useful if adults have a good knowledge of children's books so that they can recommend 'good reads'.

Screen 6/10

FRUSTRATION AND
INDEPENDENT LEVELS IN ACTION

This workshop will show you:

- that experience of Frustration and Independent levels contributes to reading development

- how to support children at their Frustration level

- how to support children at their Independent level

For Screen 6/10 redisplay Screen 6/1 – Workshop aims.

- Remind the group that three levels of reading are needed all the time. This session has dealt with two. Workshop 7 will explain Instructional level.

WORKSHOP 7

Instructional level in action

Screen 7/1 **Workshop 7**

INSTRUCTIONAL LEVEL IN ACTION

This workshop will show you:

● that Instructional level experience contributes to reading development

● how to support children at their Instructional level.

Supporting Children's Reading, 2nd edn, Routledge © Margaret Hughes and Peter Guppy 2010

PRESENTER'S NOTES FOR WORKSHOP 7

Screen 7/1: Workshop aims

● Remind the group that Workshop 5 introduced the three levels of reading. Workshop 6 focused on the Frustration and Independent levels. This session is going to deal with the Instructional level

Screen 7/2

INSTRUCTIONAL LEVEL READING: BOOKS READ WITH SUPPORT

In Instructional level reading the work is collaborative.

Children are supported as they read a more difficult book.

They receive instruction on how to tackle problem words.

They learn just how many clues they can use:

- from pictures

- from printed words

- from their knowledge of books and life.

Supporting Children's Reading, 2nd edn, Routledge © Margaret Hughes and Peter Guppy 2010

Screen 7/2: Instructional level reading

● Read out the description of Instructional level reading, reminding the group that it is on their handout from Workshop 5.

● Discuss the implication of the picture on the screen: working together. In Instructional level reading the work is collaborative, unlike Independent level reading where the child is in control, and Frustration level reading where the adult's in control.

● Stress that definite skills are required at this level of support. Therefore, point out that it may be that some parents will welcome guidance from the school. Workshop 8 touches on this.

Screen 7/3

INSTRUCTIONAL LEVEL READING: MAKING IT WORK

This level calls for a much closer working relationship between adult and child

The adult needs:

- knowledge about clues

- an enquiring mind that views reading as a problem-solving activity . . . an interest that overrides any temptation to demand word-perfection

- an understanding that mistakes are valuable, both as learning-steps for the child and windows into the child's thinking

- to be generous with praise

- the good sense to know when to end these short sessions, with the child feeling successful.

Screen 7/3: Instructional level reading: making it work

● Comment on the 'saint', perhaps as follows: 'No, you don't have to be a saint, but for work at this level you do need patience, and some degree of skill.'

● *Either* allow time for the screen to be read or read it out to the group.

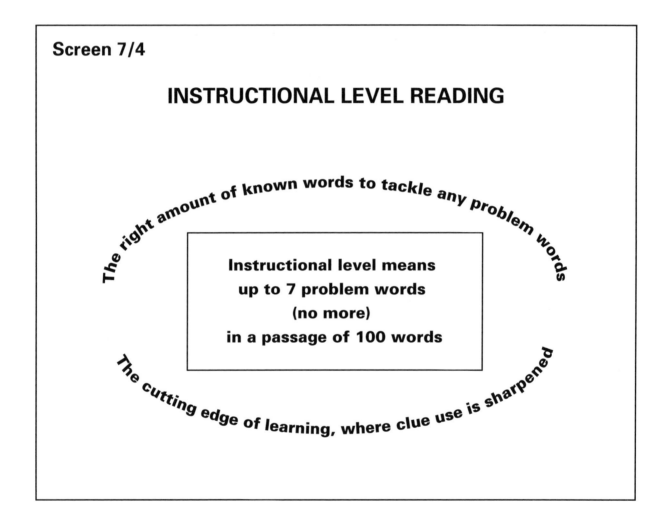

Screen 7/4

INSTRUCTIONAL LEVEL READING

The right amount of known words to tackle any problem words

> Instructional level means
> up to 7 problem words
> (no more)
> in a passage of 100 words

The cutting edge of learning, where clue use is sharpened

Supporting Children's Reading, 2nd edn, Routledge © Margaret Hughes and Peter Guppy 2010

Screen 7/4: Instructional level reading

● Comment on the name for this level – Instructional – a name referring to the direct teaching now taking place.

● Stress that it is important to keep to the ratio of no more than 7 problem words in 100, otherwise there will not be the right amount of known words supplying the clues to enable the child to tackle the problem words.

● Go on to explain that a particular difficulty arises when a few problem words cluster together. In this case, the adult should simply read most of them to the child, leaving one for the child to work on.

● Point out that they've already met examples of work at Instructional level in Workshops 3 and 4 (the scenarios illustrating the teaching tips).

● Add that the cutting-edge nature of Instructional level work means that sessions are intensive. They're hard work; they shouldn't last more than 10 or 15 minutes.

Screen 7/5

WHY INSTRUCTIONAL LEVEL WORK HELPS A CHILD MOVE ON

- It teaches children how to use clues.

- It teaches children that reading is a problem-solving activity.

- It gives them satisfaction from meeting and overcoming challenges.

- It enables children to read books beyond their Independent level.

- It offers children visible proof that they are making progress.

Screen 7/5: Why Instructional level work helps a child move on

● Explain that Instructional level work is best done one-to-one, for around 10–15 minutes.

● Point out that at school it is often possible to arrange one-to-one work. Instructional level work also takes place in planned group situations. It may also take place in class for just a few seconds for one problem word met in a worksheet or textbook.

● Explain that 'how to use clues' refers to clues both Seen (on the page) and Unseen (in your head); recall Workshops 1 and 2. Remind the group that children tend to underestimate how far they need to travel (read on, read back . . .) for clues on the page (Workshop 2), also how much background knowledge they can bring to a problem. The adult can help on both counts.

● Comment that when children realise that reading is a problem-solving activity, they change from being passive ('I can't read this, and there's nothing I can do about it; we haven't done this'), to being active ('I can get at this meaning, if I think, and search around'). This realisation has the knock-on effect of producing thoughtful, questioning readers.

Screen 7/6

SUPPORTING JOSH AT HIS INSTRUCTIONAL LEVEL

Tim got slowly out of bed. His _ _ _ _ _ _ (throat) hurt. When he washed his face, he found that his neck hurt a bit, too, if he _ _ _ _ _ _ _ (pressed) it. Tim pulled on his _ _ _ _ _ _ _ (clothes). He must get Sebastian outside before anyone saw him. He _ _ _ _ _ _ (tucked) a sleepy Sebastian under his jacket. He was just going downstairs when he remembered the box. He couldn't leave that in his room. He put Sebastian back on the bed, and got out an old _ _ _ _ _ _ (canvas) _ _ _ _ _ _ _ _ (shoulder) bag and slipped it on his _ _ _ _ _ _ _ _ (shoulder). Then he picked Sebastian up again.

Josh's problem words:

throat	**tucked**
pressed	**canvas**
clothes	**shoulder** (twice)

Screen 7/6: Supporting Josh at his Instructional level

● Introduce Screen 7/6, for instance saying: Now let's have a look at one particular Instructional session, as an example.

● Explain to the group that this is a passage that Josh was reading, in which he came up against six problem words. Four of these words will be worked on; the last two will be supplied when the adult recognises that the difficulty level is rising to Frustration level.

Screen 7/7

PROBLEM WORD 1: 'THROAT'

(JOSH halts at the word 'throat'.)

ADULT: Read on to the full stop, Josh, even though it's on the next line.

(JOSH reads 'hurt', but this doesn't help.)

ADULT: (Reads) 'His *something* hurt'.

JOSH: His t-toe hurt.

ADULT: Good! 't' for toe. You used the first letter. But look, and listen . . .
these three letters go together – 'His thr . . . hurt'.

JOSH: Throat!

ADULT: Excellent!

Tim got slowly out of bed. His _ _ _ _ _ _ (*throat*) hurt. When he washed his
face, he found that his neck hurt a bit, too, if he _ _ _ _ _ _ _ (*pressed*) it.

Supporting Children's Reading, 2nd edn, Routledge © Margaret Hughes and Peter Guppy 2010

Screen 7/7: Problem word 1: 'throat'

● Ask the group to read the 'snapshot'.

● Explain that the relevant part of Josh's text is in the box.

● After time for reading, bring out the following points:

1. Josh is reminded to read on to the full stop. (He also needed reminding to ignore the line end.)

2. The word *something* is used in place of the problem word. This avoids interruption of the flow of language, and can be given the same intonation and weight as the actual word.

3. The adult praises Josh's attempt to use phonics, then builds on that by pointing out the phonic blend '*thr*'.

4. If Josh had been unable to get 'throat', then the adult could have suggested he read on well into the next sentence, where 'face' and 'neck' provide further clues.

Screen 7/8

PROBLEM WORD 2: 'PRESSED'

(JOSH reads 'plastered it' for 'pressed it'.)

ADULT: Good! You read on. And 'plastered' could have something to do with 'hurt'. Good thinking. But 'plastered' starts with *pl,* and this word starts with . . .?

JOSH: *Pr* . . . prees . . .

ADULT: Nearly. But are you sure it's ee?

JOSH: Pr! . . . press . . . 'if he pressed it'.

ADULT: Brilliant!

Tim got slowly out of bed. His _ _ _ _ _ _ (*throat*) hurt. When he washed his face, he found that his neck hurt a bit, too, if he _ _ _ _ _ _ _ (*pressed*) it. Tim pulled on his _ _ _ _ _ _ _ (*clothes*). He must get . . .

Screen 7/8: Problem word 2: 'pressed'

● Ask the group to read the snapshot; again, the relevant part of Josh's text is in the box below.

● After time for reading, bring out the following points:

1. Josh is praised because this time he did read on to the full stop.

2. The adult has spotted a teaching opportunity. The word 'hurt' triggered 'plastered'. In saying: '*plastered* <u>could</u> have something to do with *hurt*', the adult cleverly puts Josh's thinking process into words for him. This is one way of teaching the use of context clues. So, even though the word was wrong, the adult was right to praise the working out.

3. Josh is led back to the phonics: first *pr* not *pl*, then *ĕ*, not *ee*.

Screen 7/9

PROBLEM WORD 3: 'CLOTHES'

(JOSH reads 'cloth' for 'clothes'.)

JOSH: (Puzzled) Cloth?

ADULT: It's worth taking another run at that. Read again from 'Tim pulled . . .'

(JOSH rereads, again reading 'cloth'.)

ADULT: Sometimes, Josh, there's a clue in the next sentence. (Adult reads) 'He must get Sebastian outside . . .' So, Tim's going outside. It might be cold out there. Now, Josh, you said 'clŏ'. Look at that vowel, that o. What other sound could that be?

JOSH: CIL . . . clothes . . . his clothes!

ADULT: Well done! It was clō, not clŏ, wasn't it?

When he washed his face, he found that his neck hurt a bit, too, if he _ _ _ _ _ _ _ (pressed) it. Tim pulled on his _ _ _ _ _ _ _ (clothes). He must get Sebastian outside before anyone saw him.

Screen 7/9: Problem word 3: 'clothes'

● After time for reading the 'snapshot', bring out the following points:

1. Josh is encouraged to take another run at the word.
2. When that ploy doesn't work, the adult demonstrates reading on, over the full stop and on into the next sentence.
3. The adult gives Josh a hint ('it might be cold out there').
4. Josh is then reminded to try out the different sounds possible for the first single vowel in a word (clŏ, clō).
5. Josh read this word through a mixture of context and phonics.

Screen 7/10

PROBLEM WORD 4: 'TUCKED'

(JOSH reads 'touched' for 'tucked', but carries on to the end of the sentence. He looks puzzled.)

ADULT: Good, 'touched' makes a kind of sense. He could have touched him. And the word here does look a lot like 'touched'. But what did the previous sentence tell us?

JOSH: He's got to smuggle the cat out.

ADULT: Right, he's got to hide Sebastian. And look at the picture. Now, look closely at the word again.

JOSH: Aha! 'tucked'!

He must get Sebastian outside before anyone saw him. He _ _ _ _ _ _ (tucked) a sleepy Sebastian under his jacket. He was just going downstairs when he remembered the box.

Screen 7/10: Problem word: 4 'tucked'

● Display screen 7/10 but cover the 'snapshot' so that the group see only the text in the box.

● Ask the group in twos or threes to consider what action the adult might usefully take to help Josh read 'tucked'.

● After a few moments, bring the group together to share their ideas.

● Uncover the text describing what Josh and his helper actually said.

● After time for reading, bring out the following points:

1. The adult waited to the end of the sentence to see if Josh would self-correct. Although he didn't actually do so, Josh did show he knew the sense had been lost. He is praised for this.

2. The adult again puts Josh's thinking into words for him, describing the clues used ('He could have touched him . . . the word does look a lot like "touched"'), and tells Josh there was some sensible thinking in that.

3. Josh is taken back to the previous sentence which highlights the fact that the cat must not be seen.

4. His attention is directed to the picture that shows the cat already tucked inside Tim's jacket. Comment that using a picture clue is perfectly sensible; it makes a very useful 'reserve' strategy.

5. He is invited to look again closely at the word, now he's so much more 'clued up'.

Screen 7/11

A PROBLEM TOO FAR! 'CANVAS' AND 'SHOULDER' TOGETHER

When Josh paused at the two consecutive words 'canvas' and 'shoulder', the adult told him these words.

This was done for two reasons:

- JOSH was tiring at this point, and the adult considered he'd worked hard enough.

- These were two problem words together – three problem words in the one sentence. The adult judged this a step too far . . . best to finish on a high note.

> **He put Sebastian back on the bed, and got out an old _ _ _ _ _ _ (_canvas_) _ _ _ _ _ _ _ (_shoulder_) bag and slipped it on his _ _ _ _ _ _ _ (_shoulder_). Then he picked up Sebastian again.**

Screen 7/11: A problem too far! 'Canvas' and 'shoulder' together

● After time for reading the screen, bring out the following points:

  ○ Knowing that Josh has a limited concentration span, and realising that they had already been working for almost 15 minutes at this intensity, the adult simply told Josh the words 'canvas' and 'shoulder'. The adult knew the value of finishing on a high note.

  ○ The adult recognised the important fact that this sentence, with three problem words out of 21, was now at Josh's Frustration level. (In a passage of 100 words, this would equate to about 15 words in 100.)

Screen 7/12

READING SKILLS – A MEANS TO AN END

While acknowledging the importance of reading skills, the adult supporting Josh also realises that they are not an end in themselves. They are a means to an end.

> 'Reading is much more than the decoding of black marks on the page: it is a quest for meaning, and one which requires the reader to be an active participant.'

Therefore . . .

- Instructional level sessions should begin with a little chat about the book.
- Then, as a lead-in, the adult reads the previous page, before the child reads the selected passage.
- The sessions end with some wider discussion about the book.

Supporting Children's Reading, 2nd edn, Routledge © Margaret Hughes and Peter Guppy 2010

Screen 7/12: Reading skills – a means to an end

- Emphasise that there is absolutely no disputing the fact that the development of reading skills is important for all children.
- Explain that it would be a mistake however, to come away from this workshop thinking that learning to read is about improving only the *skills* of reading. Reading skills are but a means to an end, and that end is the reader understanding what the writer has to say.
- We want to avoid children coming away from their Instructional level sessions with the notion that learning to read is only about reading *skills*.
- Explain that that is why the ideas on this screen are recommended.
- Comment on the way the statement in the box captures perfectly the marriage of skills and understanding that is reading.
- Reassure the group that this advice *is* do-able. How long you spend on each item – opening chat, lead-in reading, final chat – depends on how much time is available. For example, an opening chat could simply be 'Oh, it's *Cinderella*. Now, we've already read about her sitting in the cinders; what's next?' (Closing 'discussion' could be similarly brief.)
- **End the session with the highly practical truth that the teaching of reading skills is always more successful when embedded in content that excites, interests, amuses.**

WORKSHOP 8

It's a team game

Teaching assistant and teacher

Screen 8/1   **Workshop 8**

IT'S A TEAM GAME:
TEACHING ASSISTANT AND TEACHER

This workshop will show you:

● the importance of observation in teaching reading

● the importance of sharing observations

● how to share observations

● examples of actions based on observations

● a description of a balanced reading diet.

Supporting Children's Reading, 2nd edn, Routledge © Margaret Hughes and Peter Guppy 2010

PRESENTER'S NOTES FOR WORKSHOP 8

Screen 8/1: Workshop aims

- Comment that although this final workshop makes some reference to previous sessions, the main focus is the relationship between the teaching assistant and the teacher – an important partnership.

Screen 8/2

THE IMPORTANCE OF OBSERVATION
IN TEACHING READING

Watching and listening, in an open-minded and informed way, uncovers knowledge of where a learner is in relation to the wider scheme of what is to be learned.

The better the observation, the better the support.

Supporting Children's Reading, 2nd edn, Routledge © Margaret Hughes and Peter Guppy 2010

Screen 8/2: The importance of observation in teaching reading

● Point out that observation of reading yields its best results in one-to-one situations. Given your patience, the child's reading will reveal where he is '*in relation to the wider scheme of what is to be learned*'. This all hinges on being able to wait and see, allowing time for the child's thinking to become apparent. Mistakes are very revealing.

Screen 8/3

MEET THE TEAM

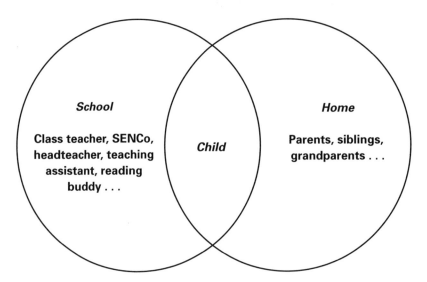

School

Class teacher, SENCo, headteacher, teaching assistant, reading buddy . . .

Child

Home

Parents, siblings, grandparents . . .

The better the sharing of observation and information, the better the support.

Supporting Children's Reading, 2nd edn, Routledge © Margaret Hughes and Peter Guppy 2010

Screen 8/3: Meet the team

- Introduce the term 'reading team', i.e. all the adults who support a child's reading in different settings and roles . . . the permutations are many.
- Explain that this teamwork can go right or can go wrong. Either the child is supported by a well-informed, unified team . . . or by several people who may mean well, but in adopting their own unique style may confuse the developing reader.

So, as the screen says, it's important that observations are well-shared through an effective chain of communication, first of all within the school, then out to other members of the child's reading team beyond the school gates.

- Stress that the teaching assistant plays a vital part in this observation process.

Screen 8/4

SHARING OBSERVATIONS: THE BENEFITS TO THE TEAM

The teaching assistant gains:

- knowledge about reading in general
- increased job satisfaction in a professional partnership.

The teacher gains:

- informed observations from colleagues and home
- a basis for planning the child's next steps
- material for reporting to home
- material for reporting to other teachers
- material for official reports.

Home gains:

- clear, up-to-date information and guidelines from school.

Supporting Children's Reading, 2nd edn, Routledge © Margaret Hughes and Peter Guppy 2010

Screen 8/4: Sharing observations: the benefits to the team

● Point out that at this stage in the workshop the focus is on benefits to the child's reading team. The benefits to the child will be illustrated later in this session.

(*Note* to presenter, regarding team relationships: see 'Diplomacy alert', page 3.)

● Explain that the next few screens focus on techniques for observing reading.

Screen 8/5

CAPTURE THE MOMENT

Feb. 12th
Marcus O'Leary
        Three Billy Goats Gruff
Page 5
Scowling
No chat
page 5 usual plod
No.
WHO'S THAT!   me ⟶ him
pr: delicious — no alternatives
                (Thumb It)
Read 2p. to him — bit happier
        p. 10 fin.

Supporting Children's Reading, 2nd edn, Routledge © Margaret Hughes and Peter Guppy 2010

Screen 8/5: Capture the moment

● The workshop so far has focused on the extremely useful chain of communication that starts with that gold-mine of information: the observation of the child reading. The big question, of course, is: how is that observation done? When a child is reading, things happen very quickly – how do I capture the important moments?

● Talk about the handwritten notes on the screen as follows:

○ this experienced teaching assistant has developed her own shorthand

○ it's an indispensable part of the job

○ it's her immediate aide-mémoire (otherwise some things would be forgotten by the time Marcus had turned the page)

○ she will need to refer to it for Marcus's next session

○ she may need it to help her share her observations, most times orally, but occasionally in written form

○ it may appear crude, but in fact it contains 'gold dust'! (The next screen will demonstrate this.)

● Imagine that Marcus's teacher was meeting his parents in the evening, but was quite unable to find time to talk to the teaching assistant during the day, to get an up-to-the minute account of how he'd read that day. So the teaching assistant leaves her some notes, based on her notebook.

Invite the group, in twos or threes, to have a go at turning these private notes into notes that would give the teacher a clear picture.

● After a few moments, bring the group together to look at Screen 8/6.

Screen 8/6

SHARE THE MOMENT

[DATE] He read pp. 5–8 of *Billy Goats Gruff*; I read pp. 9–10.

Scowling	Marcus came in scowling – his usual look when he has a book in his hand!
No chat	He offered no chat about the book, and showed no interest in my comments about it.
Usual plod	Despite ongoing work, he read very slowly indeed; this affected his comprehension.
No.	He read thro' full stops, indication of lack of comprehension.
'WHO'S THAT?'	He read the sentence 'WHO'S THAT TRIP-TRAPPING OVER MY BRIDGE?' without emphasis, until I demonstrated the meaning of its being in upper case; then he enjoyed shouting!
Pr:delicious	At problem word *delicious*, I used 'Thumb it'; Marcus unable to give alternatives.
Bit happier	I read two pages to him. He brightened up – he always enjoys listening to stories

Screen 8/6: Share the moment

- Explain that this screen shows another version of the observation of Marcus's reading. As in the exercise that they have just worked on, it came about because the teacher was meeting Marcus's parents in the evening, but had been unable to find time to talk to the teaching assistant during the day. So the teaching assistant left this account, based on her notebook.

- This up-to-the-minute account of the state of Marcus's reading enabled the teacher to:

  ○ talk about how much Marcus enjoys being read to, and to offer his parents a selection of books to take home

  ○ demonstrate how to 'Thumb it', and explain why this technique helps Marcus, asking his parents to try it in order to help him get used to reading on beyond a problem word.

- Explain that the handwritten words on the left of the screen would not, of course, appear on the note the teaching assistant left for the teacher; they are there purely to help the group make the link between the original notepad and this second version.

- Allow time for the group to read the screen.

- Point out that here the teaching assistant's observations fed into a teacher's informal report.

Screen 8/7

MARCUS: ACTION ARISING FROM OBSERVATION

Observations	Actions
Scowls	Selection of Frustration level books going home
Doesn't chat about books	
Happier when read to	Dad promising to read to Marcus more often
Plodding word-by-word style	Teaching assistant organising for Marcus to record his own reading, for playback
Lacks awareness of punctuation and print conventions	Marcus writing 'shouty' stories in class, using capital letters for all the shoutings
Lacks the reading-on strategy	'Thumb It' action being used at school in Instructional level work; parents given guidelines
Inability to come up with alternatives	GAP time

Supporting Children's Reading, 2nd edn, Routledge © Margaret Hughes and Peter Guppy 2010

Screen 8/7: Marcus: action arising from observation

- This screen shows action beginning to be put in place as a result of observation of Marcus's reading.

- Reassure the group that no one expects every single reading session to convert into such a wide range of actions.

- Point out that the next two screens will explain one of these actions, an action that may be new to the group: GAP time.

- Explain that Marcus had been unable to give an alternative word for the problem word *delicious*, in the sentence *The hungry little goat saw the delicious green grass at the other side of the bridge*, even though the teaching assistant had read the whole sentence to him, using the word *something* in place of the problem word.

- Make it clear that the ability to think of possible words that make sense in the place of a problem word is a crucial part of reading (adults do it). It's an ability that shows you understand the sentence.

- However, some children find it extremely difficult, and require extensive oral practice, with print playing no part. Unless progress can be made in this comprehension activity, their reading will be slower to improve.

- One way to give children practice in coming up with alternatives is GAP time – which stands for Give A Possibility time. The children are asked to come up with possible words that make sense in a gap in a sentence.

It can be a one-to-one activity, or group or class work.

The next screen shows this happening.

Screen 8/8

GAP (GIVE A POSSIBILITY) TIME: 1

Teacher	Group responses
Finish my sentence for me: 'I was really afraid of the savage *something*.'	beast, creature, dog, monster, teacher
OK now here's one a little bit harder, because the missing word is in the middle: you've got to hold on to two bits of information, one each side of the gap: 'The day was cold and *something*, so I put on my wellington boots.'	rainy, snowy, stormy, wet, bad
Now the hardest kind of gap . . . at the beginning. No clues to help you before you get to the word: '*Something* litter was left after the fair had gone.'	shocking, nasty, disgusting, considerable, only, lots of (*Lots of* was praised for its meaning, but reluctantly disallowed as being more than one word.)

Supporting Children's Reading, 2nd edn, Routledge © Margaret Hughes and Peter Guppy 2010

Screen 8/8: GAP Time: 1

- Emphasise that there is no print in sight in this activity.
- Explain that the group responses shown on the screen came from a group of children all observed by the teaching assistant as being in need of this activity; the work was planned by the teacher.
- Explain that here, there is just one sentence at each one of three levels of difficulty: gap at end-of-sentence, in the middle and at the beginning. In reality, the children would be given several examples of each, as needed.
- Stress that at this stage the teacher is working on improving the children's ability to think about the meaning, only.

Screen 8/9

GAP (GIVE A POSSIBILITY) TIME: 2

Teacher	Group responses
This time I'm giving you some letter clues, but just because you've got these, don't stop thinking about the rest of the sentence 'Janet's birthday is in JJJJJ . . .'	January, June, July
I'll give you the next sound: Juuuuu . . .	June, July
All right, now here comes the third sound: Jullll. . .	July!
Here's one with the missing word in the middle: 'She heard a sssss . . . sound at the door'	Strange, scratching, scary, soft, screaming, scraping, suspicious, singing, sudden, silly, slippery, sizzling
'She heard a scccc . . . sound at the door'	Scary, scratching, scuffling, screaming, scratching
'She heard a scrrrr . . . sound at the door'	Scratching, screaming
'She heard a scraaaa . . . sound at the door'	Scratching!
Now the hardest . . . a beginning word – 'Nnnnn lions came round the tent at night'	Now, naughty, nice, nine, no, nervous
'Nor . . . lions came round the tent at night'	Naughty
'Norm . . . lions came round the tent at night	Normally!

Supporting Children's Reading, 2nd edn, Routledge © Margaret Hughes and Peter Guppy 2010

Screen 8/9: GAP Time: 2

● Make sure the group notices that now the examples include initial letter sounds, but again remind them that this is purely oral work.

● Explain that this is the same group half-a-term further on. Before they come to this addition of initial sounds (phonemes), children may need considerable practice with meaning-only examples.

● Point out that this activity trains children to hold the meaning of a sentence in mind while using phonic clues. Remind the group of earlier sessions in the course, about the balance of Seen and Unseen clues.

Screen 8/10

A READING TEAM THAT GOT IT RIGHT

Sam's readingful day: a balanced reading diet

	Independent level	Instructional level	Frustration level
School			
Home			

Screen 8/10: A Reading team that got it right

- Display Screen 8/10 and ask everyone to make a quick copy on their notepad of the grid on the screen (or provide copies).
- Explain that now they are going to hear a story about Sam and his reading team, a team 'getting it right'. (The story appears overleaf.)
- Ask the group to keep a tally of Sam's experiences at each level, at school and at home, by putting a tick in the appropriate box as each experience is named in the story. They should be able to see how balanced Sam's reading diet is.
- Read the story overleaf.
- Allow opportunity for any comments.
- Draw attention to the importance of the last paragraph of the story ('So – Sam's readingful day was achieved . . . every team member contributed differently, yet importantly'), to finish on a high note.

Note: Just as there will have been opportunities for discussion within the eight workshops, it will now be equally important for related discussion times to become part of the ongoing routine of the school.

Sam's readingful day . . . the story accompanying Screen 8/10

Sam's teacher read to the whole class a science text about the Beaufort Wind Scale (Frustration level), then read Rosetti's *Who Has Seen The Wind?* (Frustration level), involving them in comparing the language in each reading. Sam read quietly to himself for two five-minute periods, one just after morning registration (Independent level), then again as the afternoon session began (Independent level). As one of a group of six, he worked with his teacher to supply some of the words deleted from a shared text at the group's Instructional level. He went with a volunteer helper for a one-to-one Instructional level reading session during his afternoon's work.

At home, his mum was able to find time, that day, as soon as he arrived, for reading together. Today his book from school was at his Independent level, so he read it all through to her, and they had a good laugh at some of the pictures. Mum then suggested that he read it to his younger sister, because the pictures were so funny, so he got another go at reading the whole book. Gran came round later, and she had a new comic for him. He loved the strip cartoons with their speech bubbles (Independent level), and Gran read the full-length story to him (Frustration level), and also helped him to read a couple of jokes on the jokes page (Instructional level). At bedtime it was Dad's turn, and he read a book with press-button sound-effects – *The Hunchback of Notre Dame* (Frustration level).

So – Sam's readingful day was achieved without it being too onerous for any one adult, his teacher included. His balanced experience came from good teamwork. Every team member contributed differently, yet importantly.

Appendix

READING OBSERVATION SHEET

- As shown in Workshop 8, the day-by-day observations of an informed teaching assistant are nuggets of information far too valuable to lose. They can feed into the school reading-record system.
- The following Reading Observation Sheet (ROS) is an example of one such system.
- The ROS should be printed as an A4 leaflet. (Print A3 double-sided, and fold.)
- The inside left-hand page (Reading Reactions) deals with attitudes to reading, the right-hand page with reading skills (Use of Clues).
- The fourth side may be left clear for other observations and notes.
- The photocopiable pages of the ROS (p. 166–71) are followed by copies of the two inner pages completed with sample comments; for the purposes of demonstration, these comments refer to a number of different children.
- All these observations are geared to the planning of next steps.
- This is why it can be just as useful to enter a 'No' or a 'Sometimes' as it is to enter a 'Yes'. For example, for No. 6, 'Reads on and returns to a problem word': 'No. Tom read on . . . and on . . . and on, making no attempt to return, with enormous loss of comprehension.'

READING OBSERVATION SHEET

Pupil's name_____   Age_____

Date started_____

Class_____   Teacher_____

TA/Reading Buddy_____

Material read:

Use this same sheet to record reading over several observations (for example, half-yearly).

Make your dated entries in different colours.

Use material at Instructional level

Supporting Children's Reading, 2nd edn, Routledge © Margaret Hughes and Peter Guppy 2010

READING REACTIONS

1. Initial attitude:

2. Whilst reading . . .

   [a] makes comments:

   [b] asks questions:

   [c] challenges/evaluates:

   [d] non-verbal responses:

3. After reading . . .
   – pupil initiated response/action:

USE OF CLUES

4. Uses high frequency words efficiently:

5. Rereads up to problem word:

6. Reads on and returns to problem word:

7. Gives reasonable 'alternatives' to problem word:

8. Uses phonics to choose the correct 'alternative':

9. Uses context to fine-tune reasonable phonic attempt:

10. Uses initial phonics to trigger a word:

SAMPLE COMMENTS: READING REACTIONS

1. Initial attitude:

Marcus came in scowling; asked 'Do I have to?'
Josh's opening comment was 'It's good, this.'
Lisa mentioned she had read other books by the same author.

2. While reading . . .
[a] makes comments:

'They're having chips. We're having chips.'
'That wizard's not very houseproud.'
'This book's only got 16 pages.'

[b] asks questions:

Interrupted his reading with 'Eh? Why are they doing that?'

[c] challenges/evaluates:

'He should have cleared off when his dad got mad.'
'I don't get this. It doesn't make sense.'

[d] non-verbal responses:

Chuckled.
Wanted to go on reading at end of session.
James yawned, sighed, rocked on his chair.

3. After reading . . .
– pupil initiated response/action:

'Can I draw a picture of it.'
'Have you got another one by her?'
'Now can I make my own little book about dinosaurs, like this?'

Supporting Children's Reading, 2nd edn, Routledge © Margaret Hughes and Peter Guppy 2010

SAMPLE COMMENTS: USE OF CLUES

4. Uses high frequency words efficiently:

There were no high frequency words among the words Jeevan couldn't read.

If Poppy gets one content word wrong, she misreads the following words, even if they are high frequency words that she's learned.

5. Rereads up to problem word:

Yes. Chris uses this strategy every time, now.

Emma-Rose could pick up the sense from my rereading, but only once did she do it for herself.

No. Gemma stopped dead at each problem.

6. Reads on and returns to problem word:

No. Tom read on . . . and on . . . and on, making no attempt to return, with enormous loss of comprehension.

Sometimes. Fred's aware of this principle, and can do it in simple sentences, but can't retain larger units of meaning in more complex sentences.

Pippa never thinks of going past a difficult word.

7. Gives reasonable 'alternatives' to problem word:

Silas read 'tackle' for 'equipment' in the sentence 'Anglers need the following equipment.'

George read 'noises' and 'sounds' for 'cries' in the sentence 'They have heard strange cries at night.'

8. Uses phonics to choose the correct 'alternative':

George eventually read 'cr-ies' after previously supplying 'noises' and 'sounds.'

Jessica corrected 'terrified' to 'scared' in the line 'He was scared of the dark.'

9. Uses context to fine-tune reasonable phonic attempt:

She changed 'hug' to 'huge' once she had read to the end of the sentence 'He gave him a huge box.'

Baljit persisted with 'prŏt' for 'protect', without taking any notice of the sense, in 'You must protect seeds from the frost.'

10. Uses initial phonics to trigger a word:

He combined minimal phonic sampling ('str . . .') with context, to read 'straight', in 'Sally went straight home.'

Yes. Massimo built 'sub', then immediately read the whole word 'submarine', in 'The submarine went down under the black water.'

References

Workshop 5, Screen 5/5, etc. (the three reading levels)	Betts, E.A. (1957) *Foundations of Reading Instruction*, New York, American Book Company.
Workshop 6, Screen 6/8 ('the literacy club')	Smith, Frank (1987) *Joining the Literacy Club*, London, Heinemann.
Workshop 6, Screen 6/8 Workshop 7, Screen 7/12 ('Reading is much more than the decoding of black marks on the page . . .')	Cox, Prof. Brian (1989) *Report of National Curriculum Working Group for English*, London, DES.
Workshop 8, Screen 8/2 ('Watching and listening in an informed way . . .')	Guppy, P. and Hughes, M. (1999) *The Development of Independent Reading*, Buckingham UK and Philadelphia, PA, Open University Press/McGraw Hill.

Further references for the theory underpinning *Supporting Children's Reading* are to be found, under 'References' and 'Related Reading', in *The Development of Independent Reading*, Guppy, P. and Hughes, M. (1999).

The examples of children's readings ('snapshots', and others) are taken from the authors' teaching records. (All names have been changed.)